Friendship

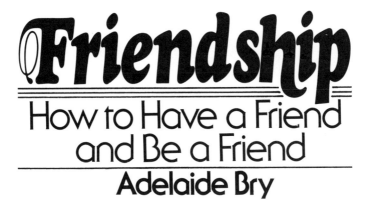

Friendship

How to Have a Friend and Be a Friend

Adelaide Bry

GROSSET & DUNLAP
A FILMWAYS COMPANY
Publishers • New York

These friends provided a special contribution to this book: Sassha Brooke, Marylee Goldberg, and Len Snyder.

To John Avrutis, a True-Blue Friend

A very special acknowledgment to my friend Judi Miller, who took time out from her tap dancing lessons to share in the writing of this book.

If you're ever in a jam, here I am.
If you're ever in a mess, S.O.S.
If you ever feel so happy you land in jail,
I'm your bail.
It's friendship, friendship,
Just a perfect blendship,
When other friendships have been forgot,
Ours will still be hot.
Lahdle-ahdle-dig, dig, dig.

If you're ever down a well, ring my bell.
If you ever catch on fire, send a wire.
If you ever lose your teeth and you're out to dine,
Borrow mine.
It's friendship, friendship,
Just a perfect blendship,
When other friendships have ceased to jell
Ours will still be swell.
Lahdle-ahdle-hep, hep, hep.

—Cole Porter,
from "Friendship,"
Dubarry Was a Lady

Contents

Chapter I
Do You Take Friendship for Granted?

"The feeling of friendship is like that of being comfortably filled with roast beef; love, like being enlivened with champagne."

Boswell's *The Life of Samuel Johnson*

Funny, how we take friendship for granted, isn't it? But when you stop and think about it, you can read your life as a book. Each chapter has its key friends. A best friend who lived across the street and was a grade school playmate. A high school friend, someone you could share your feelings about the opposite sex with. Then in the next chapter, your best friend becomes involved with a girlfriend or a boyfriend and you don't. You feel left out. Hurt. And so the personal book of your life continues.

Just for a moment, review quickly your cast of characters—single out those special people to whom you were attuned, who seemed to connect, who would listen to your troubles and care, whose troubles you cared about, who made the world a lighter, brighter place.

Looking back, wouldn't you agree that we do tend to take something as basic as real/true friendship for granted, when we have it? During times when we must

1

do without it, we tend to feel there's nothing we can do. New friendships will just happen naturally. I am suggesting that there is nothing magical or mystical about friendship. You can do something about the friends in your life, or those you wish in your life, by simply knowing more about what friendship is and being aware of your life in relation to your friendships. Knowledge will add delight; ignorance will keep you on the same old paths.

I, too, took friendship for granted the way most people do. I, who always had a friend to go bicycling with, a friend to wheel the baby carriage with, and friends to share the daily ups and downs with, discovered the importance of friendship—when I found myself without it. Just this past year, after nearly a lifetime in Philadelphia, I chose to spend six months in California. I went with telephone numbers scribbled on little pieces of paper. Friends of friends of friends, in some cases. I thought it was a clever idea at the time; little did I suspect that those little pieces of paper would be my lifeline. I had no idea what it was like to be really lonely until I went to California. For a long while, my only human contact was the waitress at the coffee shop and the man at the newspaper stand in my hotel.

Then I realized what my reality was. Friends didn't magically appear; they didn't just happen. I forced myself to dial all those faceless names on my slips of papers. Yes, I was shopping for companionship. It was difficult. More difficult than I had ever dreamed. But it was better than the gnawing loneliness I could feel eating away at me. I did call every single name. Many were busy; others opened their hearts—immediately.

At that time, it occurred to me that friendship, the ease of it, is not something to be taken lightly—nor for granted. Because, after breathing and eating and sleeping, friendships are essential to our survival. Even the

rare human being who becomes a hermit must have some
contact with the outside world. Thoreau, it is said, inter-
rupted his solitude every once in a while to hear the sound
of a human voice as opposed to the chirp of birds. Very
few people are totally independent of others no matter
how convinced they may be that they are. In fact, as the
divorce rate soars, many of us are more dependent than
at any other time in history upon friendships that truly
work for us, bring us joy and give us a sense of well-being
and belonging. We need someone who cares when we're
sick or upset or have good news to share.

My California Dial-a-Friend System worked. I began
to meet people and actually formed several close friendships that spring immediately to life now when I visit California. I wonder now how many people go to a new city
armed with phone numbers to help ease the loneliness.
No matter how you approach friendship, it involves putting yourself on the line. Risking. Saying: I'd like to know
you, I'd like to offer my friendship.

I learned the value of friendship by trying, for a short
while, to exist without it. By knowing what it's like to be
lonely. Truly lonely.

Loneliness—The Other Side of Friendship

Loneliness means different things to different people.
Let's very quickly distinguish between *loneliness* and
aloneness. They are almost opposite states of mind.

In aloneness, you *wish* to be alone. You feel peaceful
sitting on the beach by yourself, listening to the waves
crash against the sand. Or you enjoy switching on some
music, mixing a drink and relaxing, alone. You can be
busy in your aloneness. Activities such as painting, clean-
ing out your closets and writing poetry are creative alone-

ness. Aloneness means taking *space* for yourself. Giving
yourself time to reflect, slow down, sort things out. Most
of us find we emerge from periods of aloneness feeling
refreshed. I know that I find answers to questions that
were brewing but wouldn't come to mind because of the
static of too much daily input. Aloneness can be nourish-
ing.

Loneliness can be depressing and frightening. Loneliness may mean going a whole weekend without talking to
anyone but a grocery store clerk. Loneliness can also arrive smack in the center of a large, lively party. Late night
talk shows cater to people who call in just to talk to someone, anyone. In New York City, Chase Manhattan Bank
had a long-running successful advertising campaign: "You
have a friend at Chase Manhattan."

William A. Sadler, Jr., author of *Existence and Love*
and sociology professor at Bloomfield College in New Jersey, has devoted a great deal of time to the study of loneliness. He conducted workshops throughout the United
States, in which people came together to share their
views on loneliness and work in groups to transcend it.
Professor Sadler says, "As I come to understand loneliness more and more, I see it as an experience of depriva-
tion. That's one reason why loneliness is so painful. Because people do perceive themselves as being deprived
of something they think is terribly important. That feeds
into their self-esteem so that they feel as though they're
failures and unwanted."

To be lonely seems to be a condition of epidemic pro-
portions in America. We're in a very mobile era. People
are relocating more often than at any previous time in our
history, losing families and friends in the process. Our
ancestors who came to this country knew their homes
would be broken and knew that other attachments would
have to be formed. So individualism in America has been

with us for a long time. And today we are living even more our individualistic lifestyles, but we want, we need, relationships to save us from the empty vacuum of separateness. There is the terrible separateness of our own lifestyles, careers, apartments, and lonely cars driving down the highway.

If this seems dismal, it has nevertheless motivated people all over the country to get to themselves, to discover the value of friendship. Friendship is becoming the New Movement. Friendship workshops are mushrooming in cities throughout the country. National magazines offer an article about some phase of friendship or loneliness almost every month or so. Friendship as a topic of discussion on college campuses is replacing sex. Students seem to have had their fill of the sexual goodies available to them in this permissive era. They have reached the honest conclusion that sex may be the least intimate thing we do. That friendship has longer value for the heart. That it may be the real cure for loneliness.

Many people go into marriage, a relationship, or even sex, thinking it will dispel loneliness. But, just matching bodies doesn't do it. One young man found out how wrong this concept is. A well-dressed, bright, up-and-coming corporate comptroller, he confided, "I thought marriage was the total answer to this loneliness I feel. Not so. I love my wife but the loneliness hasn't disappeared. And I find that disappointing." His complaint is not uncommon. Sometimes I have the feeling that a lot of what passes for love these days is really loneliness and the hope that mating will chase it away. Totally too much expectation on *one* relationship.

The only real and lasting cure for loneliness is communication. Open, true, feeling communication. That takes truth. And truth is the cornerstone of real friendship. There it is. Until the day you are willing to reveal who you really are to someone you trust, you will not have those real friendships you want. You will probably always feel lonely.

How Do You Define a Friend?

C. S. Lewis in *The Four Loves* gives a beautiful interpretation of friendship: "This love, free from instinct, free from all duties but those which love has freely assumed, almost wholly free from jealousy, and free without qualification from the need to be needed, is eminently spiritual. It is the sort of love one can imagine between angels."

Stimulated by this poetic definition, I asked the people I interviewed in the course of writing this book just what they thought a friend was. I then emphasized that I did not mean a casual friend, but a true, real, best friend. No questionnaires were used. People presented their answers from the top of their heads without intellectualizing first.

To the question "What is a friend?" came the following replies:

> Someone who'll always be there when you need them.
>
> Someone who will do something for you without asking for anything in return.
>
> Someone I trust implicitly; whom I would go to in happiness and sadness.
>
> Someone you can really unload to.
>
> Someone you feel at ease with, who knows your mind and your moods.
>
> The person you're married to or living with because that's the person you take your day-to-day problems to.

Somebody I can trust with the inside of me.

Someone who knows you are a no-good son of a bitch but loves you anyway.

A wife that sticks with you for twenty-eight years even though you're a nut.

Someone who is able to accept your growth and development.

Someone you can count on as a true friend even though you may know them two months, not twenty years.

Someone who is honest, patient and willing to see you through the good as well as the difficult times.

As I explored friendships, it struck me over and over again that friends are the essence of our lives. People thoroughly enjoyed telling me about those human beings who added sparkle, enjoyment and meaning to their lives. I also noted the emphasis on the real friend, the friend I call the True-Blue Friend. That is the person who speaks the truth and listens without judgment or criticism. That is the person who, when the chips are down, can be totally depended upon and trusted. Or, equally important, when things are going our way, is genuinely happy for us.

You don't have to play games with a friend. You don't have to pretend you are someone you're not. A friend is a person you can count on . . . and who can count on you for emotional support.

What about the question of economic support? How does money affect a friendship? Some people feel that borrowing money is an infringement on a friend and doesn't do anything to improve the self-reliance of the person who is asking for help. I asked several people, "Would you loan money to a friend?" I got heavy, emotional answers—both no's and yes's. I can't give any black-

and-white answers to this big question, "Do you loan or
don't you?" because there are no right or wrong answers.
When the situation comes up, you will have to trust your
gut feelings.

But I will add this, because the question of money often
does arise in a True-Blue Friendship: Certainly, if this
person is a real rock-bottom friend and loaning money is
no more inconvenient to you than lending your car for the
day or donating a container of milk, then there is no problem. But, for most of us, money is fraught with so much
significance that it might be wise to treat it in the most
objective, nonemotional, businesslike way possible.
Don't be hurt if your closest friend is reluctant to loan you
money. For money isn't just money, and that's the problem. It is hate, fear, love, all of those things. When you
touch someone's money button, you may trigger a whole
raft of connecting emotions. All of which may not be as
tragic as you think. Your friendship stands a chance of
becoming even closer by a very real examination of the
feelings a money problem can evoke.

Until now, we have been, more or less, using the word
friend as a generalization. But there are levels of friendship. It is knowing those levels that will set you straight.

The Kinds of Friendship

How many times have I heard it said, "I feel betrayed
by _____. I thought _____ was a close friend. Well, let
me tell you what _____ did!" I've heard it said and I've
said it myself from time to time.

There is no betrayal. Never. Ever. We merely fail,
sometimes, to see the friendship for what it is. We wear
blinders because it suits us to have the friendship.

Here is the crux of friendship: learning to determine

just who is and who isn't a True-Blue Friend. Then, learning to enjoy the other friends in your life for what they
are, for what you share with them, for any length of time.
Do not confuse the different types of friendship, or yes,
you will feel betrayed; yes, you will be hurt.

Let us make these three basic distinctions: True-Blue
Friend, Casual Friend, Friendly Acquaintance. There
are even more subdivisions, which will be covered in
depth in Chapter III, but for the purpose of making a
point, let's concentrate on these three types of friends.

We all have our own ideas of what True-Blue Friends
should be. They make you feel good and warm; they are
automatically on the same wavelength; they feel genuinely sorry and come to your assistance when you're in
trouble; you can speak freely to them, you don't have to
be on guard; they really listen; they care about what
you're doing . . . the list could go on and on, though it
would vary for everyone.

A True-Blue Friend is a joy in our life, unless we find
with a painful jolt that the person wasn't true-blue. But
how can we know that before we get hurt? And, sometime
or other, most of us do get hurt. Or, what if the other
person considers *us* to be more of a friend than we really
are? Should we feel guilty? No. You do not have to put up
with unsatisfying friendships and neither does the other
person. I will help you judge whether a person is a True-
Blue Friend or not.

Look over the qualities I have given a True-Blue
Friend. Make some additions, if you like—or subtrac-
tions. Now, let's pull one of the qualities from the list, for
starters, and examine it. No doubt, "they really listen" is
on your list. Let's analyze this business of listening. It can
be tricky. Our cliché is: A good friend really listens when
you speak. The truth is: Some people go through life as
very convincing listeners. They might actually be a mil-

lion miles away. Friends you think are listening may only look that way. How can you tell? It's not that easy, but you can watch the look in their eyes, the gestures of their hands and body, any flicker of animation in their face.

In other words, they may be listening, but they don't *hear* you. Certainly no reason to end a friendship, but a valid clue that they are not the kind of friends to you that you think they are.

If you are talking on the phone, stop in the middle of the conversation and introduce something totally ridiculous. This is a sneaky trick, but brings immediate results. You might be relating a story about your car breaking down in the middle of Highway 26 in pouring rain when all your credit cards were in the pocket of your raincoat hanging in your front-hall closet. Quickly switch to some gibberish about Humpty Dumpty and the cat jumping over the moon. If the person doesn't inquire as to your sanity, you know he or she isn't listening. And it could be one clue, among many, that you have misinterpreted the friendship. If you are asked what in the hell you are talking about, make a little joke, "Oh, just trying to see if you were listening . . ."

If you find your friend hasn't been listening, what other qualities on your list of True-Blue Friendship have you misinterpreted as well? A True-Blue Friend must pass all these tests, or most, with flying colors. You will know, finally, in your heart, after you become more aware of what friendship is, who is and who isn't a real friend. To test the reality of friendships is to test your understanding of friendship.

The most common friendship division falls between friends and acquaintances. But there always seem to be people who fall somewhere between. They're not close friends, yet they're not just acquaintances, either. I call these people Casual Friends, and the category can include passing acquaintances and friends who are almost close for a time. They come and go in our lives with greater frequency than True-Blue Friends, but during their stay they are more meaningful than Friendly Acquaintances.

If you admit you have trouble sorting out True-Blue Friends from lesser friends, ask yourself the following questions. Take each question and keep one friend in mind at a time. If to any of the questions your answer is yes rather than no, the person is more a friend than an acquaintance. If there are a number of yes answers, the person is probably a True-Blue Friend.

Separating-an-Acquaintance-from-a-Friend Quiz

Can you stand each other after several drinks?

When people drink they become uninhibited and truths come spilling out as fast as the liquor is poured. Do you and your friend embarrass each other? If you are really friends, you will know the truths and you can merely say, "Oh, c'mon, you're just drunk." The same principle applies if either of you gets silly, sloppy, sentimental or sassy. You're still friends.

Can you spend time together, comfortably, without talking?

Friends don't always need activities to share time together. They can share the silence; they can do their own activities, sharing the space. If you've ever sunbathed with a group of friends—some dozing, some reading, some doing needlepoint, some in quiet thought—you know the feeling of friendship meant here. It also means not being driven into a panic if there are long lapses in conversation.

Can you express angry feelings to each other?

There is no law that says friends can't become angry with each other or have differences. But the way to keep the friendship solid is to express those feelings. You don't have to shout nor do you have to berate. Simply be truthful with your friend and tell him or her why you feel angry. Then, forget it.

If something nice happens to you, will your friend be genuinely happy?

Many people told me they wanted friends to share their griefs *and* their joys. But not everyone will be "happy for you." Remember, a True-Blue Friend will not be jealous of your triumphs, will not say, "Please, I can't stand hearing about your successes," but will be genuinely happy you are happy. Any friend you can't share good news with and rejoice with, because he or she envies your good fortune, is not a True-Blue Friend.

Does your friend remember your birthday?

If your friend doesn't call for a while, do you feel worried rather than insulted?

Probably you can think of other questions to include. To be really honest, why not test yourself to find out what kind of friend you are? Did *you* remember to send your best friends birthday cards? Do you stand on ceremony and avoid calling when a friend hasn't called and you feel it's not your turn?

Writer Susan Witty moves this difficulty in distinguishing who your friends are into a clearly identifiable light in a humorous essay in *Harper's* magazine (August 1973, "Friendship," wraparound section).

> You wake up in the morning next to your best friend, your husband. It's a beautiful morning.

. . . While you're making toast, he tells you for the 25th time how to apply butter. At the table you ask him for the 50th time to please stop cracking his knuckles. It's wonderful to have someone to share things with.

As soon as you've cleared away the breakfast things, your neighbors Edith and Bill drop over for morning coffee. You can't figure out what this friendship is all about, since you don't have anything in common with them, but you cheerfully launch into the same conversation you always have, keeping the stream of meaningless chatter going as best you can. . . .

When the fresh morning sun has stolen away and is replaced by the deader heat of midday, the four of you decide to go and visit Ed and Sandra, another couple you've all spent many happy hours tearing apart behind their backs.

She then goes on to talk about the hurtful and old, unresolved jealousies when the group chooses up sides for a game of soccer. After leaving the "friendly" game of soccer, she and her husband go for a quiet walk and bump into an old friend from work who holds her job in his hands. Not trusting him for a minute, she nevertheless invites him over for a drink. Fortunately, he thinks of an excuse not to accept. She ends her day with:

Your husband wants to walk east and you want to walk west, so you go your separate ways, arriving home just in time for dinner. As you're about to sit down, the phone rings. It's your oldest friend from childhood. She keeps you on the phone for an hour and a half telling you her problems. Throughout the conversation, she keeps calling you Sylvia, the name of another one of her friends. You don't want

to cut her off or criticize her because you're afraid
she'll get angry and a friend from childhood is very
rare. You start to give her advice, but she remembers something she has to do and hangs up.

You've missed dinner, but before you go to bed,
you sit down to write to a pen pal who has never
written back.

It's been a full day and as your head hits the pillow
you wonder what you would do without your
friends.

A satirical portrait, but we chuckle because it has the
ring of truth. It is not always true that we will find out who
our real friends are in a disaster. The fact that a friend is
not True-Blue sometimes becomes evident in times of
great success.

Steven Spielberg, producer of the movie *Jaws*, admitted candidly, "Friendship and loyalty are two of my
most cherished values. I have a lot of friends who turn
away when you achieve success. Some acquaintances who
I thought were my friends turned into snipers when *Jaws*
hit the top. I'm leery—really cautious. I don't make
friends that easily because I think a lot of people don't
know what it means to be a true friend: how to recipro-
cate, how to share the bulk of the problems, how to be
honorable."

Though we aren't all celebrities, surely we all have our
private successes. Do you have a friend who would turn
away if you got that promotion, moved to a nicer neighborhood, got married? (More about the Success Syndrome in Chapter VII.) And the Failure Syndrome is a
valid test as well. Will some of your friends drop you if
you lose your job, sink into a depression, get a divorce?
Do they want to be bothered with you if you are not UP,
UP, UP?

It should be very clear by now that you can't lump all your friends into the same friendship bag. Here is a quick slide rule to sort out who goes where: Friendly Acquaintances (people you can stop and chat about politics with); Casual Friends (people you can argue about politics with); True-Blue Friends (people with whom you rarely talk about politics, unless it is a special interest, because the two of you have so many other things to talk about).

Once you understand and learn to recognize the different levels of friendship you will go a long way toward protecting yourself against the deep hurt of a Fairweather Friend, the quirky inconsistencies of a Bar Buddy, or the cool distance of a Historical Friend.

Where Friendship Begins

With your mother. Your first contact on this planet. It then widens to include your father, the rest of your family and the neighborhood.

Preview of a Future Cocktail Party

My curiosity about the beginnings of forming friendships took me to a nursery school near my home. There I sat like a giant in a tiny chair watching fifteen preschoolers go about their business in life, which is playing and learning to play with one another. As I observed them, noting how their individualistic personalities were already clearly etched, I thought of this little poem I had heard somewhere:

> *Friends are a lot like cakes*
> *Some are devils*
> *Some are spicy*
> *Some are lemons*

Some are icy
Some are nutty
but very few are perfect angels . . .

Why did this folksy ditty choose to buzz through my
mind at that moment? Most likely because little children
are rarely subtle or sophisticated. They are easy to read
and I could see very precisely what kind of friends they
would eventually grow up to be.

They started out in a sloppy circle singing their start-
the-day songs. All eyes appraised me, the giant. I saw
long hair, tousled hair, blue eyes, sleepy eyes, happy
smiles, cranky frowns. My mind played tricks as I envi-
sioned them all at a cocktail party around the year 2000.
For like the adults I know, some were fearful, sitting just
outside, some held hands and smiled at each other, and a
couple of children eyed each other warily.

While the group was singing "Three speckled frogs sat
on a speckled log" I noticed one little boy, sandy hair,
freckles, off in the corner—just watching. The teacher explained to me later that his name was Danny and he re-
fuses to join the group, but sometimes will venture a little
closer to it.

Over in the sandbox, Sarah, hair in her eyes, was fu-
riously throwing sand at an intruder who had infringed on
her territory. She raised her voice to a screech, indicating
where and how the other child might play with her. "A
controller," I mused. In years to come she would take
charge, controlling others who were willing.

Then there was Jennifer. A buttercup blonde who
looked like a tiny all-American cheerleader. Jennifer was
a little older than the rest, a little taller than the younger
ones, but she was not yet ready for grade school. Every so
often she would yank one of the smaller children away
from play and cuddle the child as if he or she were a live

doll. The teacher informed me with a smile, "Oh, yes, Jennifer is our little mother." I could see Jennifer with her grown-up friends, watching out for them, doing favors, giving, giving, and often getting nothing in return. Apart from the instant stroking she supplied—and sometimes the children pulled away from her—she remained distant. She really was not playing. She had already learned that her friendship role was "nice mommy." Constant giving does not make an ideal friendship. Far from it. Friendship needs the interplay of give-and-take to be truthful. But there are a lot of grown-up Jennifers playing "nice mommy" because it makes them feel needed and liked.

I glanced over at little Danny again. His thumb was jammed aggressively into his mouth as he wandered aimlessly from paintboxes to puzzles to the cage that housed the pet birds. I could see him in about twenty-two years pouring out his heart to a therapist, telling about how lonely his life was—without friends.

You can span a lifetime, literally, and find the same types of personalities in nursing homes. There are the Dannys who appear to be outsiders, the Sarahs who play cards with gusto but control the game—yes, there are similarities between nursery school and nursing homes. If nothing happens in between.

It's those in between years, though, that concern us. For when it comes to friendship, it is simply not true that you cannot change. You are not merely a person who has been programmed and conditioned through experiences that have brought you to your present point. You do not have to be run by your past. You can open up *now*. Right now. You can learn to discriminate. You can enjoy a wide circle of friends and acquaintances. But it will take thought and doing. The Dannys, the Sarahs, the Jennifers—all can learn to have real friendships.

Hey! This Is Me!

One way to begin is to start being who you really are by opening up and being truthful about yourself. A good test is to observe the language you use. Just listen to yourself speaking to others. Does it sound like a politician's language? Polite, well-chosen, even fancy words that don't really say anything because they don't mean anything. This is one way people put up barriers to prevent themselves from really being who they are.

Let's take the example of Howard. Howard was a master at appearing amiable, a good listener, a regular guy. He was the perfect corporate type. Howard lived by a personal credo: "Don't offer any true information," he once said. As a matter of fact, that was as personal as I remember Howard ever getting with me. He never did offer any information. He answered questions in a vague sort of way. Everything was done so skillfully, you wondered what really made Howard tick. There was no possibility of a give-and-take friendship because Howard couldn't, or never learned how to, give. He never got angry; he was sweet; when he lied, he always covered it up beautifully.

I concluded there was a lot missing in our friendship. Howard wasn't there.

It's quite likely my former friend has never been truthful with himself or with anyone else. He doesn't acknowledge hurt, anger, any of the feelings he is actually experiencing with people. He has programmed himself to keep things on an even keel, to be civilized, and that means keeping his true feelings from friends.

No, I can't be real friends with the Howards of this world. Real friendship is impossible without truth. You may have to be the first to tell the truth. It helps others to open up.

Truth can't enter into a friendship, though, if you are not truthful with yourself. Are you? Here's a test: A good friend stands you up for a lunch date and keeps you waiting in the pouring rain. Would you be furious? Yes, even if it were your nearest and dearest friend. Even more reason to be angry is that you may have been worried. If he or she does not have an acceptable excuse, would you say just how angry you are? Or would you say, "Oh, that's okay." It's truthful to show anger to a friend if that's what you feel. It's part of being yourself.

The way to openness and truth does not require heavy soul-searching. Just remember to *be yourself.* Forget that huge sense of separateness we've all inherited and start reaching out to more people.

The Circle of Friendship

Try this exercise: Think of friendship as a mammoth circle. The word *friendship* follows the curve. Within that circle of friendship are written the names of all your friends, interspersed with the words *love, joy, laughter, annoyance, agitation, anger*—all the human feelings you can imagine.

Now, for fun, take a person you consider a good friend and put that person in the circle, along with your feelings. Close your eyes and see the big circle of friendship, the name of the person and all the feelings you associate with that person.

Love. Anger at the way that person sometimes acts. Withdrawal when he or she acts that way. Everything. Let yourself be totally honest about this.

Now ask yourself if you have actually shared the whole range of feelings you feel about this person you call a friend. If you can permit all the emotions you have privately admitted feeling about this friend to come out in the open, you will improve your friendship enormously— *if* you do it constructively in the course of the friendship.

Then switch roles and put yourself on the line by imagining how the other person feels about you. Once these imagined feelings are brought into friendship and expressed, friends can truly share experiences. That's what makes up a True-Blue Friendship.

Telling the Truth

So many people I interviewed discussed truth. That person hadn't been truthful with them. This person *is* truthful. Truth is so integrally a part of friendship. So many of us have been burned by friends we have thought deceived us in some way or another. It hurts. We expect, almost demand, that friends be truthful with us. But we must be truthful, too—with them and ourselves—and that, in essence, is the key that will unlock any friendship door.

Needless to say, by truth, we are not talking about giving our unsolicited opinions or endless advice or self-therapeutically expressing whatever pops into our minds. The truth we do mean is—not playing games. That means shedding the disguises and letting the *real* you come through. It means not lying to the other person but, mostly, not lying to yourself.

Perhaps the kind of truth we mean in a friendship is best expressed in this poem by Bertha Conbe:

> *Every friendship*
> *that lasts is*
> *built of certain*
> *durable materials.*

The first of these
is truthfulness.
If I can look into the eyes
of my friend and
speak out always
the truthful thought
and feeling
with the simplicity
of a little child,
there will be
a real friendship
between us.

Unlimited Friendships

There's an old cliché that says, "You can count your real friends on one hand." This may or may not be true for everyone, but there's nothing to stop you from having many kinds of friends. Not all will be of the True-Blue variety. You might have a friend to play tennis with, a friend to go shopping with, a friend to rehash old times with, a friend to discuss literature and music with. And more. A mixed friendship bag can be yours.

One of the biggest mistakes we all make is to expect all those friends to be packed into one person and labeled "My Best True-Blue Friend." Quite often, this is impossible. Not to mention dangerous—what happens if that person moves away, or worse, dies?

It is much more sensible and fun to have friends on several levels. Your True-Blue Friend may just happen to loathe the opera or football or not be into meditating. If you have these interests, why not share them with other friends? Attend the ballet with one friend, then go home and call your True-Blue Friend and tell that person what the doctors said about your tests because that friend is waiting to know.

My credo on friendship is fairly simple:

> I know that I am willing to take the responsibility for being truthful and telling the truth.
> I believe in having many friends since they help me to grow and learn.
> I realize that I will outgrow some friendships. They will sour or weaken and maybe disappear as time passes by. If and when the time comes to part, I will wave good-bye with love.
> I know the differences between the many kinds of friendship, so I won't get hurt by those differences.
> I know that the word *always* when used in the context of friendships is a long, long time and I'm content with living in the now.
> I know my friends are a reflection, a mirror, of who I am now, and I might find myself changed one day.

My credo was created to by yours. Add to it, change it, make it your own.

There is one other point I want to add because it never ceases to amaze me how people change. You may have been shy as a child and a loner as an adolescent, but as an adult you can bloom, anytime. You can enjoy many friends whenever you are willing to. You can open up. And once you become truthful, it's hard to go back to the old ways.

Once you understand friendship, stop taking it for granted and learn more about the friends you have, you will find that you have a certain loving control over the quality of friendship in your life. For it doesn't "just happen." When you take the mystery and mysticism and "taking it for granted" out of friendship, you will make better friends and be a better friend.

Chapter II
How to Get a Friend and Be One

"The only way to have a friend is to be one."

—Emerson, *Essays,*
  First Series: "Friendship"

If you take friendship for granted or feel it just happens, consider the following: Is there any other area in your life you just let happen—your career, your education, your love life, your children's rearing? Odds are, no. They take work. Friendship, too, takes work. But, assuming that everyone has a friend, or friends, why should we even bother to read or think about friendship? Because our lifestyles are changing swiftly. Right now, they are not anything like those of our grandparents or even our parents. We move more frequently, we have access to a greater variety of people, we grow and change in many ways that weren't possible before.

Because of this, we need to expand our ways of thinking about friendship. We can create friendships, save friendships, permanently or temporarily, end them—even put some on "hold." We *choose*. If a friendship is not forever, it can still be a wonderful thing.

24

Being a Friend

We are all fairly explicit in what *we expect* from our friends, but have you ever stopped to wonder what kind of friend you are? You know the questions to ask yourself. The obvious ones. Are you considerate, do you listen, are you a "good" friend and so forth. But I am going to come down hard on truth and ask you to ask yourself—are you a truthful friend?

Being truthful can be difficult. We are so used to fudging, pretending or even lying, a lot of which comes from our childhood when we were afraid to tell the truth to our parents so we lied to save ourselves.

But we are adults now. How do we speak up? When? I leave the "when" up to you, hoping it will just flow when you understand the "how." Keep this in mind: *Whatever you feel, whatever your truth, it will not hurt as long as there is no blame attached to it.* When you simply tell the truth because that is what you want to do, without making the other person wrong, merely to share yourself, it will work. If you blame, it won't.

You can start practicing the truth in the privacy of your bedroom. Say the truth into a tape recorder and play it back. It might be an expression of appreciation or something truthful about someone you don't like but have never really admitted before. You may feel awkward and timid at first, but keep repeating this exercise. Record, play, rewind, record.

I can remember when it was so hard to tell the truth my heart would pound. I was scared, but I practiced and it worked. I noticed this recently with a friend. I said, "You haven't called me lately, is anything wrong?" She confessed, "You ignored me when I had my bad back and had to stay home." If I hadn't shared *my* truth with her at that moment, our friendship might have hit a snag that could have lasted for years. Maybe forever. I risked it by venturing the truth. Then I discovered the hidden truth in her mind as well.

Being a friend also means being a friend to yourself. It's really okay to like yourself. Love yourself, it you wish. A loving individual always cares about him or herself. This is number one. This is not an ego trip. This is not narcissism. This is not being selfish. If you think self-love sounds egotistical, remember the idea is found in the Bible: "Thou shalt love thy neighbor as thyself." When you stop to think about it, if we didn't love ourselves, we would be self-sacrificing masochists or faceless clods waiting to fall into the hands of someone who would promise to shape us into a better image.

Self-love does not mean you sneak looks in a mirror whenever you find one. Nor does it mean you brag about yourself. Self-love means liking yourself and knowing yourself well enough to even love what you call the "bad." Another way of saying self-love is self-esteem.

You might have days when you are very proud of yourself. Like the day you mastered jumping off the high diving board. Or when you managed to pull yourself through a bad depression after a love affair soured and you emerged having learned something. Or you love yourself because you're busy and happy and love life. The bottom line is you love yourself because you're here and alive. That's all.

If you can say honestly that you do not love yourself, ask yourself why? Did your mother constantly remind you that you were a disappointment? Did your father make it clear that you were no great beauty or scholar or talent? Are you afraid to open up to people because you think if people saw the "real you," they'd run? Do you identify with Groucho Marx, who once said, "I wouldn't want to be in a club that had me for a member"?

If you don't love yourself, it will reflect in your friendships. Chances are you will select friends who have the same low self-image. Then the chain reaction starts. You are not truthful. You talk behind each other's backs, enforce the mutual belief that you have bonded together because you are losers and no real trust or love can fight its way through.

Just to see how much you do, or do not, love yourself, make a mental list of those qualities you don't like in someone you call a friend. Write them down if it's easier. Now check off exactly how many of those so-called negative qualities you think you possess. I've used this technique with groups of people and for some the shock is immediate. What you do not like in the other person looms right there in you!

Some people appear, on the surface, to have a fine self-image but their choice of friends is a giveaway. For all their friends are confused, self-destructive or totally helpless. Friends do reflect what we see in ourselves. They are like mirrors. So, unless these people are dedicated do-gooders, you could wisely conclude that they do not love themselves. They need the feedback or worship from people they consider their inferiors. This makes them look good. Satisfying friendships are impossible for them.

Most of us do have a healthy measure of self-love, but in certain situations our insecurities backfire on us. Take the question of the friend who hasn't called. You have noted that it is his or her turn and you flatly refuse to call first. What exactly is taking place here? You are angry with that friend for not thinking you are important enough to remember. Which brings us back to self-love. Another way to look at it is—"Why, I haven't heard from Ed in a week. *I'd better call.* He might be in trouble. Or, if he's having a ball, I'd like to hear about it." Still another way to handle it is the truthful, friendly way: *ask*. "I don't know if you realize it, but I seem to always call you. I'm beginning to wonder—is there a reason?" A question like that, of course, would *not* be presented in an accusatory way. It's just a simple query.

If your self-esteem is quite low, please don't punish yourself. For I assure you, it can change and improve in time—if you are willing to grow and learn about yourself. Here's one good exercise to begin with: When you wake up in the morning and self-doubts begin to creep into your consciousness even before your morning coffee is poured, say to yourself, "Uh oh, here come those negative thoughts again." Then see them written in the sky above your head like a skywriter's puffy writing. Watch them disassemble in the sky and float off into the distance so you can't make them out anymore. Don't aggravate yourself by fighting the negative thoughts. Let them come up. But when they do, let them go and watch them in a nonjudgmental way.

Do you wait until your self-esteem has improved before searching for friends? Absolutely not. You might wait forever! When we understand friendship and pick friends who reflect the best in us, we reinforce our self-love. This self-love, then, gives us the energy to express our love of our friends. It's an endless cycle. Think of waves that wash onto shore and roll out to sea again. We all want to find friends who reflect our self-love. How do we go about this?

How to Get Friends

First, let's do some collective soul-searching. Dr. Herbert Otto, a friend who is chairman of the National Center for Human Potential in La Jolla, California, believes that most people are wallowing in what he terms "friendship delusion." We think about our closest friendships that no longer exist. We refuse to admit, now that we have grown up or moved away, that good friends are actually gone. We keep remembering old friends, good times. Consequently, we fail to face up to the reality, the *now*. We may actually have no real sharing, caring friends in the present. Some of us would do anything for those old friends, but they may be far away. This is a familiar lament of recent college graduates whose friends are scattered. So don't delude yourself. When you think of who your friends are, don't think in the past. Those are friends that *were*. You want friends that *are*.

You want friends who can share the laughing and the crying, now. Friends you can talk to often, friends to go places and do things with. But they won't just happen.

The easiest way to begin finding friends is to make a list of all the qualities you find desirable in a friend. Len Snyder, a psychologist who has conducted friendship workshops, urges people to put anything they want on the list. To let themselves feel free. Here is a list he made, to give you a sample. He is truthful:

1. I don't want friends who are overly fat. I know this is not tolerant of me, but this is my right and my prejudice.

2. I like people who are generous with their emotions. I don't consider myself particularly uptight so I enjoy being with real people who laugh easily, cry if necessary, and even get angry. I like men who are not afraid to touch, even hug if they feel like it.

3. I think it's stimulating to have friends at all levels. I have a friend who's a truck driver. We have a few

beers and talk together every so often. He's not a best friend, but we found a common meeting ground and enjoy talking.

4. I like friends I don't have to see every week or even every month. If I am terribly busy or pressured, why can't we pick up, say, after Easter where we left off when we met for a drink on St. Patrick's Day?

5. I like to talk about our friendship directly. How is it working? Is it okay with the other person? I like to have these things out in the open.

How would your list read? Draw one up. You don't have to agree with anything on Len Snyder's list. Robert Townsend, an English professor at Amherst College who has organized friendship projects, would definitely disagree. Being friends with someone from a totally different walk of life *sounds* nice, he feels, but isn't always possible. "I think this is one of the very bases of Aristotle's argument," he says. "That you have friends who are equal. I think when power or class becomes a factor in a relationship, friendship flies out the window. This business of trust and equality are essential to me."

He also has difficulty talking about a friendship directly with the other person, number 5 on Len's list. If that sounds odd, it is only because we are not accustomed to talking about friendship quite so seriously. Actually, people in love relationships make similar boundaries all the time and discuss the parameters endlessly. How do you feel? Would you say to a friend, "How do you feel about our friendship? Are there any things you would like to change?" Would you say, "Would you mind not calling me after ten P.M. anymore? I'm going to bed early so I can get up early and jog before work"?

"Shopping" for the Right Friends

We all make a mental list when shopping for potential lovers or mates, though we may not be conscious of doing so. One man seeks out his "type." A tall, willowy woman with melancholy eyes and a Renaissance face. A woman shops for Mr. Right. He has to be virile, intelligent, and do something interesting. The point of all this is that we rarely think of prospective friends with half as much mental effort as we use thinking of lovers or mates. And yet friends may last longer.

Make your list, tuck it away and, a few months later, when you have collected some new friends, take it out again and check it. How close did you come to hitting your target? Did you find friends who did not match your exact specifications, but discover that it doesn't much matter?

Sassha Brooke, a California therapist and good friend of mine, has also done work with friendship in groups. These groups were born of her observation of a quite accepted but unnecessary habit. "I saw many patients," she said, "who were dedicated to their therapy long after there was any real need for it. They were simply there to share their secrets, joys and tragedies on a per-hour basis with a 'purchased friend.' Therapy was no longer necessary, and I thought they would get more value out of group sessions that helped them form friendships."

Sassha decided to incorporate some of her somewhat reluctant ex-patients into more structured groups that dealt with making and recognizing friends. Sassha's groups also started with a list. The list specified not what they wanted in a friend but what they were not getting from their current friends. This list is designed to point out what you need to do about your friendships and in what area.

Here are Sassha's questions. What are *your* answers to them?

Sassha's Friendship-in-Focus Quiz

1. Check out right now how many people you see each week in your life. Don't forget people who are not necessarily real friends—co-workers, elevator men, the grocery store clerk you stop to chat with, friends you play a sport with, friends you meet for lunch, friends you might call long-distance, and your True-Blue Friends. Think of everyone with whom you really interact in an average week.

2. What kinds of things do you like to do when you get together with your special friends?

3. What would you never, ever reveal—even to your best friend?

4. What do you enjoy talking about most? What's a "good/juicy/gratifying" conversation for you?

5. What kind of information is okay to share with your friends, but only your close friends?

6. How many people can you really count on in an emergency? Men—how many are women? Women—how many are men?

In jotting down your answers on paper, you should be able to see your own conclusions forming. For example, maybe you thought you had lunch out several times a week, when actually you've been eating at your desk more often than you realized. Or, you find that most of your leisure time is spent alone. Perhaps, too, you have very few opposite-sex friends and none of them are good friends. This quiz is meant to show you where there might be gaps in your life when it comes to friendship.

Sassha advises her groups, "Go after friends. Your whole life begins to change once you begin to act on friendship instead of letting it find you."

She encourages the members in her group to call up anyone they can think of—a friend at the office, an acquaintance from an old office, a new neighbor, as many people as they know or have just met—and make plans to get together. These are weekly "do it's," or Rx's, as she calls them.

One young woman began by timidly making three phone calls per week. After three weeks, she had two new luncheon companions. At the end of the fifth week, she had a new boyfriend, because through her new friends she began to make other friends and got invited to parties she would never have been invited to otherwise.

Follow the procedures Sassha instructs her groups to use. Deliberately cultivate new people. Take the initiative and accept the risks that go with it. Yes, you may get rejected and you may never know why. But you are putting your life into motion. Risking is the only way. From that comes the reward.

Where to Find Friends

Many people moan and groan about the lack of friends in their lives, not realizing that they are doing everything possible to *prevent* themselves from meeting new people. A female patient of mine once took apart every detail of her daily schedule and we found the problem right there. Her day consisted of driving to work, parking her car and nodding hello to the parking attendant, going to her office where she does research, eating a sandwich at her desk during lunch, burying herself again in her projects, leaving the office at five, nodding good-bye to the receptionist, picking up her car and going home.

While you probably won't be able to match her rigid schedule—the only two people she made contact with were a parking attendant and the office receptionist—analyze whether you have become something of a "lifestyle shut-in." In the winter, do you tend to hibernate at home? Do you make an effort before weekends and holidays to plan something with friends? There is no secret to meeting and making new friends. Just the simple common sense of five little words—*Get out and do it!*

You may be familiar with the get-up-and-get-out instructions given singles. All of that doing and going and participating also works for making friends. You can make friends in adult education courses, political activities, in your apartment or in your neighborhood, even in a bar. There are bars, such as dart-game bars or neighborhood hangouts, where the atmosphere is friendly rather than competitive, as it is at certain singles bars.

Sporting events are a good way to meet people. But keep in mind, if your team is playing for "blood," you won't meet as many friends as you would if the game has an element of good fun and teammates tend to go out together afterward. Parties are a good way to meet people. For some it's a breeze; they seem to be equipped with a natural confidence, or poise. Or self-love. For others, parties are a private torture chamber. What do you say? What if you find yourself sitting alone with no one to talk to? Everyone's talking but you. You're frozen until you or someone makes a move. What does everyone think? You know they're all staring at you and it's so embarrassing!

It may be comforting to know that everyone has felt this way at some time. Who knows—even the people with the biggest grins, the loudest jokes, who seem the *most* at ease. Here is a lesson that should help you get through any similar circumstance and I sincerely hope you write it down and never forget it. It's just this: *No one is even noticing you. They're too busy concentrating on themselves.* What you think is your glaring awkwardness cannot be seen like a neon light. Your insecurities are not noticed; no one can see. This knowledge—and I assure you it's the truth—should help you relax at your next party or anywhere. It will also help you to concentrate on the other person, and there is no better way to meet and make friends than that.

But I'm shy, you might say. Discovery of shyness has become very popular lately; reams of material have been written about it. I can't get excited about the subject of shyness because I think shyness is an involvement in oneself. Torturous as it may seem, we can shed it. By breaking through that delicate eggshell we label our shyness, we can begin to look at the world with self-love and confidence. We do this when we stop thinking of ourselves so much. We do this while we are with others. Remember that everyone is fearful to some degree and we all hide in the house of shyness. Chic clothes, a biting wit, a loud voice—they're all expert covers. But the best cover of all is to forget about yourself and concentrate your attention on the other person. Then we lose our shyness and gain self-love.

When you do find yourself standing alone at a party or similar social occasion—no need for panic. Simply go up to a person or enter a group and be there. If it is one person, you might want to ask a question or make a comment that will begin the conversation. Remember, that person is also *standing alone*. Say whatever happens to come to mind about, perhaps, the situation you find yourself in. "Are you a friend of the hostess?" is an example. If you want to meet people and you are open, you're bound to meet them and maybe make new friends. This can happen at parties, sporting events, club meetings, even in the supermarket or while walking your dog. Finding friends is not so much the result of a technique as of a friendly attitude.

Corporate wives (as well as army wives and doctors' wives) could probably give lessons on taking the initiative in making new friends because of the frequency of relocation in their lives. Joyce, married to a doctor, has spent her husband's internship, residency, army stint, and change of specialties in six different cities in the space of fourteen years. She almost shudders to think of again collecting cardboard boxes for packing and saying good-bye to dear friends. Her first move when she arrives in a new city and her children are placed in schools is to go out and meet the neighbors. She joins women's groups, throws birthday parties for their children (inviting their mothers for coffee), volunteers her services and takes pottery classes. Joyce does not have a lot of time, either. In addition to running the house and taking care of the children, she has a part-time position teaching psychiatric nurses. But no matter how busy she is, she has learned not to be too busy to make new friends. Though, admittedly, she longs for the day when she and her family will settle in one city for longer than a few years, she sighs and makes the best of it, joking, "Well, at least it's not Saudi Arabia or Moscow."

A woman of fifty I met in San Diego moved there from the Midwest, where she had lived for thirty years. She had recently divorced her husband and arrived knowing only two people. She sat down one lonely evening in the small apartment she had rented—a vivid contrast to the spacious home she had owned and where she had raised four children—and told herself she had two choices: one, she could be alone; two, she could plan her own support system. (And those are the words *she* used.)

She told me, "I need a lot of people in my life, not just two friends. So I decided on a plan of action. First, I went to the local hospital and volunteered. Then, I took a course in the evening and deliberately made an effort to talk to men and women after class. After a month, I decided to invite a group of women to meet in my home once a month to discuss anything and everything. It worked so well that two years later it is still operating. The women come and go but the core is the same.

"I also decided to approach men as people, not as potential dates, affairs, future marriage partners. I have made firm friends with men. And, about once a month, I call about a dozen people, not necessarily an even number of men and women, for a potluck dinner."

She also joined the Unitarian Church because she felt its members would be on her wavelength. She met a wide variety of people. Now, two years later, this woman is literally inundated with friends. Out of a group of around one hundred people, she has three close women friends and four men friends.

I sat across the table at the dinner party where I met Doris, in complete admiration of her. She knew what she needed to make her life work and had gone about organizing it, as one might a business. When we look for a job we make a similar effort. We know one is not going to come to us and that there is a certain ratio of success. So it is with friendship.

Age holds no barriers, either. Mr. and Mrs. Moss of Columbus, Ohio, looked out the window one cold day in a typically severe Midwestern winter and decided the time had come to retire to a warmer climate. They chose Phoenix, Arizona. Arriving in the summer with a few phone numbers, they experienced some loneliness until

fall, when clubs and organizations got started again and
they could join and meet people. That was three years
ago. Edith Moss said, "I got up every morning and considered how to make friends. I called two people a day."
Far from being homesick for Columbus, they think of
Phoenix as their home. They have friends now. This is a
couple who are past sixty-five and who left family and
lifelong friends to start a new life. Though it used to be a
rule that people become less flexible as they get older, it
isn't anymore. Not in our Move-Around Society!

No matter where you go or how you choose to meet and
make friends, your attitude is the key. Do you, truthfully,
ever think the following:

> I feel so out of place.
> I don't know how to make friends.
> I never knew how to take or make compliments.
> I just know they'll never like me.

If attitudes resembling these are fixed in your mind,
you will radiate them. People will pick up on them.
Watch the negatives in your mind and then go back to
concentrating on the people you hope to meet. And concentrate on the people as you meet them. Again (and
again and again), the irony of this kind of negative thinking is that it's such a waste. *Remember*, other people are
too involved in themselves to take note of your insecurities.

Courtship of Potential Friends

Friendship, C. S. Lewis wrote in *The Four Loves,* is
born at the moment when one person says to another,
"What! You too? I thought that no one but myself . . ."

A friendship might be born at lunch between two women who find their lives are similar. Two men start talking at a break in an evening course they are both taking and find they have much in common. How do you define potential friends? Very easily. It starts with something you discover you have in common. One indication is how fast the conversation flows when you first meet. You find you are kindred spirits. When that happens, drink it in. Enjoy the moment you are sharing with this new human being in your life.

After the magic, the work begins, because many times we say, "Here is a fun person; we'll have to get together, meet for lunch," but we never do. Taking these magical moments for granted makes us forget how rare they are, and out of habit or laziness we neglect to make our moves, only to regret it later.

The very next time you spot or sense that magic, think of the words on this page, look your Potential Friend straight in the eye and suggest lunch or dinner, or coffee or drinks, or whatever, immediately. As soon as you both can make it. Or, if you prefer, take a few moments right then to form a tiny seed for a friendship that could blossom and grow. Say simply, "Hey, you and I have a lot in common. I like you. I'd like to be friends."

How seldom we express those beautiful appreciative words that will warm the other person through and through, more than any electric blanket or fabulous fur. If you appreciate the person, tell him or her. Whenever that magic sparks, grab it and help it grow.

Dr. Otto and others have commented on how much our history affects us. The unique thing about potential friends and forming friendships is that you don't share a past history. Your mutual history is just beginning. Your personal history is part of the past, and the past is always gone. Instead of sharing histories, why not share a new kind of rootedness: experiences.

Dr. Otto gives an example, a recent experience with a potential friend of his. He suggested they visit a local art exhibit since they both love art. They stopped along the way and bought the usual outdoor junk food fare—pizza, ice cream, soft drinks. The two men had such a good time, they decided to make the Westwood Art Exhibit an annual outing.

"Afterward," he says, "we went to dinner at a superb restaurant, something I consider a rare treat. This person is in the process of becoming my friend and we had a terrific time. There is a type of rootedness here. We took part in experiences, which gives each a warm, happy feeling. We shared enjoyment and fun."

You don't have to do anything *special* to have a shared experience with a friend-to-be. It makes it more fun, but the sharing is the actual experience.

Tips for the Very, Very Busy

"It's easy for other people to talk about making new friends and keeping up with friendships," someone told me, "but you don't know what my life is like. I'm so busy right now I'm lucky if I have time to sleep, let alone take my clothes to the cleaners. How can I go after new friends?"

We all have periods in our life when we carry a full workload. Perhaps we go to school and work, have a new baby or are rushing to meet a deadline in our work schedule. The pressures of day-to-day survival must come first.

But we make time for romance and sex, don't we? Couldn't we also squeeze in a *little* time for friendship? Leigh, a freelance illustrator, solved the dilemma this way: "I truly live under the cliché—feast or famine. When it's feast, I have no choice but to gear all my forces and get the work done. Each time this happens, my friendships take a backseat to my deadlines. I always feel something is missing in my life, but I never know what to do. There's always so little time. Of course, I still get together occasionally with my good friends, but I have no chance to develop new friends. I discovered recently one way of solving this. Just a few phone calls a week to friends I had met, but hadn't developed because I was busy. My reasoning was that most of them worked and had to eat lunch, as did I. I made time to arrange just one lunch date a week. Not the best way, but the best I could do. And it adds so much."

Margie, a young housewife from Cleveland, married in her mid-thirties after a full dose of the swinging singles scene. She then proceeded to have two babies almost one after the other. Determined not to be a typical housewife and suffer from "cabin fever," Margie hired a babysitter every Thursday. She thought she deserved one day off from a full-time job. At this time, she gets together with friends, away from the interruptions and demands of the children. They go shopping or have lunch or just walk around together and talk. Margie's motto, ever since I have known her, has been: "One can never have too many friends." And she lives by it. Her friends are very important to her.

Perhaps because of career priorities, many men complain that it is far easier to find dates than make male friends. A man who relocated to San Francisco from New York complained to his friends back home he just couldn't make friends with men. He didn't know how to go about doing this. It had always just happened.

At an est graduate training seminar, a forty-seven-year-old man who was a multimillionaire admitted that he had no friends. He watched TV or slept for hours on weekends. He understood that his problem was the fear of being vulnerable. Open. Revealing himself. Many men have similar fears, not only of being vulnerable or weak, but of the threat of homosexuality should they form close friendships with other men.

This man, Bob, said, as he turned to look at me squarely, "I couldn't have said this even one year ago. I thought all men who had close friendships were queer."

Bob does belong to the forty-and-over group in which homosexuality is more threatening than it is, say, to a young man in our more open era. But men can and do put aside these fears and form close friendships.

Robert Townsend's professional interest in the subject of friendship stems from a period in his life when he needed to take the initiative. He was newly divorced and very lonely and found himself thinking a lot about friendship. Ingeniously, he decided to meet with a group of men who had had similar experiences. It was not a men's consciousness-raising group, though they did meet regularly once a week. It was also not for business reasons. In fact, they set a rule about that. If one started talking about his profession, he could consider himself copping out. The group was there for support.

"It started," he says, "when I just went around to men I knew in comparable positions and asked them, 'How would you like to have a meal a week?' It was out of bewilderment, loneliness—and you can fill in the rest.

"The very fact of a group of men having lunch together every Friday, when the week was coming to a close, without an agenda, without falling back on business or shop talk, is quite extraordinary, I think. I started this group in New Haven and then began a new one when I came to Amherst. This time the men were married and we sometimes met in couples. There's a degree of explicitness and openness when we do meet in coupled situations that I've seldom experienced. But the basic group of friends is really the five or six men who meet for lunch regularly."

If you are very, very busy, you are very, very busy. But, ask yourself, are you also very, very satisfied with your life? If you feel something's missing, perhaps stopping now and making some time for friendship might be the best thing you've ever done, the best pattern you've ever formed. Use your imagination. Release yourself for just a few minutes from your Busy Person role and use the time to make a phone call or meet someone. Make lists if you have to. Devote a little time to friendship now and you might stay off the path that may someday lead straight to loneliness.

As we get older our lives do become more complicated, but our approach to friendship needn't be. Ever watch children playing in a playground? I call young children playing "a party." Recently I sat on a bench in a playground in California and just watched. One little boy kept approaching a little girl who had a bright, shiny shovel and pail he wanted to play with. He kept trying to be included in her game and she kept pushing him away. The last time, she held out her hand, and putting the pail and shovel aside, they dashed off to the swings together.

How simple. And how beautiful. For how can a two-year-old know the meaning of the word *rejection?* It simply does not exist. He just kept trying to be the little girl's friend. At four, his life will be more complicated. At ten, he will only make friends with little boys. And at twenty-five, he may be so busy he won't have time to make friends. When he's rejected, he'll wonder why.

The secret, I think, to forming friendships though you may be very, very busy is to keep it simple, as a child does. The more we can contact the inner kid inside ourselves, the more we can reach out and contact people and

the less of an effort it will be. If you have a hectic schedule, make a little effort without a lot of heavy thought.
Just being and sharing with someone you enjoy will do.
Or, as a Zen master once shared with his disciples, "Enjoy
a leaf together." That is the secret.

How Far Can You Go in a Friendship?

Jeffrey, a man I know, loves to go fishing. A relaxing
hobby for a sometimes wound-up intellectual and a welcome break from the pressures a university professor is
under. He likes to go fishing with one man, a professional
fisherman. It is a friendship based on shared solitude and
talk about how the fish are biting and the weather. Jeffrey
would never dream of bringing the intricate struggles of
university life onto the boat. One day, however, he
overstepped the boundaries, going into deep waters
where he should have traveled with only a fishing rod.

On this day, he had just had one of those unfinished
fights with his wife, Meg. His mind was fragmented.
When he lumbered up to his friend's boat, the fisherman
took one look at him and said, "What's the matter?"

Jeffrey needed desperately to talk to someone so he
blurted out, "I'm having problems with Meg."

Then he recalls, "He looked at me, and I never forgot
what he said. He said, 'Listen, Jeff, I'm just a simple fisherman. I don't know anything about woman problems.
But I do know whatever is eating you, this boat will do
wonders to take your mind off it. Now, let's have a good
day of fishing.'

"I shut up fast. I mean he was so right. But when I got
home I called my friend Harvey, who loves to listen, is
extremely sympathetic and has had these problems. We
met at a nearby pub."

Jeffrey learned a valuable lesson in the art of friendship that day on the boat. It's simply this: Some friends are for one thing; others are for another. Don't go too far with the wrong one or you will make that friend feel uncomfortable.

Two women simultaneously complain about a mutual male chum of theirs they met while working in a public relations firm. They both hear from him once a year, when he has a problem on the job or wants to change jobs and expects their support. During the rest of the year he contributes nothing to the friendship. He may be best described as a friend who is heard from only during the bad times. Then he calls and unloads on them both. "It's like a pattern," one woman says. "To tell the truth, I'm getting tired of hearing it. It's hard to be sympathetic after a while." The second woman agrees. "I would say, yes, he's gone too far now. Too many jobs, too many times."

Going far, but maybe not too far, in a friendship also extends to the need to express love and warmth in a physical (but not sexual) way. The hugging, the kissing and the touching. Some women do this easily. So do some men. Not too long ago, I witnessed two men who had known each other from childhood put their arms around each other, touch, and clap each other on the back. It was very moving. It was very fluid and happened naturally in the course of the evening. For many men, though, this closeness will never happen. Though European men have been kissing and hugging for years, American men are inhibited by the fear that any gesture might be interpreted as a homosexual one.

Bill, a man who once shared this belief, described to me a warm, intimate evening he had had with a male friend. They had gone to a bar for a drink and he found himself opening up and really talking to this person. Talking about problems in relating to women in a way he had

never been able to before. Then the conversation bal-
looned into even deeper subjects. Bill had found a True-
Blue Friend and he was ecstatic.

Upon parting, he clapped his new friend on the back
and shook hands enthusiastically. Then he embraced him
quickly, impulsively. Out of the corner of his eye, he
spotted someone he knew walking on the other side of the
street. It was an office colleague. For a moment, he wondered what the man must have thought. And then something happened inside. He just refused to surrender any
more to that old stigma. He had found a friend and expressed himself truthfully. That was all that mattered.

Susie, a twenty-five-year-old former patient of mine
and victim of the sex-on-demand singles scene, once re-
counted to me her sexual relationships over the year. She
remembered only ten; the rest were one-night stands.

Funny thing was, she admitted, the sex wasn't her
main objective. She loved the touching and being held.
One man, when he detected this, accused her of wanting
to be a little girl. Susie had, at that point, begun to think
about her lifestyle. She realized the touching she required in sexual relationships was a poor substitute for
the real friendships she wanted in her life. She found herself snapping back at this man, "Damn right, I like being
touched and held. Is that a sin?"

A lot of changes have taken place in America in the last
fifteen years. Like Europeans, we are now becoming a
"kiss, touch, kiss, touch" people. *Women's Wear Daily*,
the fashion newspaper, coined a phrase some years back.
They called all this "the Cat-Pack Kiss." A tongue-in-
cheek phrase for the obligatory kiss we are now required
to give in the name of friendship.

Not everybody cares for all the kissing and hugging.
Norma, a young woman with a past history of too many
orders to "kiss grandma and grandpa hello, kiss your aunt

good-bye," is plainly weary of all this. "I can't stand it when the kiss comes. Yes, I kiss back. But it seems so meaningless to me. I prefer kissing certain friends on certain occasions when it's straight from the heart. Doesn't have to be anything special, but it's not that phoney-baloney stuff."

Professor Robert Townsend, a man certainly not afraid to express genuine affection with his men friends, agrees with Norma: "I think a lot of the hugging and kissing is bullshit. You get the feeling everyone is saying, 'Aren't we rich in feeling?' and they have daggers in their back pockets. At least foreigners have ritualized it as a pattern of their social behavior. I think you can feel the difference when the kissing and hugging is real and when it's not."

Ask yourself what's appropriate with your friends. Who would be offended and who would be touched. And be natural.

One way to solve the problem of how far you can go in your friendships as well as what friends you'd like to make or already have is to really understand what types of friends there are. They do fall into categories. Many of your friends, True-Blue and Not-So-True, may be representative of types found in the next chapter.

Chapter III
Your True and "Not-So-True" Friends— A Classification

"The best elixir is a friend."
—William Somerville,
  The Hip

I want this book to give you a deeper understanding of friendship and a more practical way of making it work in your life. To do that you have to know who your friends are and what kind of friends they are. Many of the friends you have now or will meet will fall into a category of friendship. Some may overlap. Some may be in the process of changing. Seeing the varieties should give you more insight into your friendships.

You might want to keep a pencil handy while you are reading so you can analyze your friends on the basis of this list. The following types of true and "not-so-true" friends will be explored:

    True-Blue Friends
    Historical Friends
    Bar Buddies

Your Ex-Lover
Dumpers
Platonic Friends
Office Friends
Pygmalion Pals
Triads
Friends of Friends
Jewish Mothers
Long-Distance Friends
Gay and Straight Friends
Convenience Chums
The Old and the Young
Special-Interest Friends
Fairweather Friends

True-Blue Friends

These are your best, true, real friends who are with you in the good times and the bad, who are magically on the same wavelength.

"Janice is my very best friend. She's a lot like me. Even at school, when the other kids have their Twinkies and all that stuff, I know that she has health food in her lunch box and we can eat together. She *knows* me and who I am and that makes all the difference in the world." Elise, student, aged ten.

The True-Blue Friend. What the poets write about. Through thick and thin, joy and sorrow—the True-Blue Friend. Some of us only have a handful of such friends, but that's okay. When they pass out of our lives, they're hard to replace. Sometimes harder to replace than lovers.

I think a good description of True-Blue Friendship is

found in the Bible. Ecclesiastes 6:14–17, which in the
New English version reads:

> *A faithful friend is a secure shelter;*
> *Whoever finds one has found a treasure.*
> *A faithful friend is beyond price;*
> *His worth is more than money can buy.*
> *A faithful friend is an elixir of life. . . .*

That seems to capture the essence of True-Blue
Friendship. It's a secure shelter when we're with our
True-Blue and, yes, faithful friend. We look forward to
the phone chats, our activities together or just spending
time doing nothing, maybe not even saying much.

"Whoever finds one has found a treasure." I am truly
sorry for anyone who hasn't experienced the joys of the
True-Blue Friend. That person is lonely, indeed.

"A faithful friend is beyond price." We can't buy a
friend, nor can we compute a friend's worth in dollars and
cents. The "elixir of life" is our faithful, best, True-Blue
Friends who prolong life by enriching it.

A True-Blue Friend possesses some of these qualities:

Nonjudgmental: He or she accepts you for what you are
and doesn't tell you what or what not to do. You *feel safe*
with this person, and this feeling of having a "secure shelter" is at the center of True-Blue Friendship. The best
story I ever heard about True-Blue Friendship involved
a man who had a friend who went to jail. His friend was
neither a mugger nor a rapist nor an arsonist. He was a
broker who, in a bind, invested money illegally. His
friend had no idea he was in jail. But when he called his
office and found out, he drove twenty-five miles one early
Saturday morning to see him. He was told he couldn't get
in because too many family members were visiting the

man. The next Saturday he started out again and this time was told he would have to apply for a pass. The third trip offered another obstacle, but he kept trying only to find that the man was too ashamed to see him. He ignored that and went in treating the visit as if they were meeting in a coffee shop. When the broker was let out on parole, the two men continued their friendship. When the broker was able to talk about his experience, his friend listened. No questions were asked, no judgment was passed. Certainly the man who was in prison felt safe with his friend.

Feeling safe cannot be described in words. You will recognize this feeling when it exists. As you understand friendship, you will learn how to know this state. One of the basic errors of friendship is being mistaken about this.

On the Same Wavelength: You might disagree about a political issue, or one of you will be a vegetarian and the other won't, but basically you share the same *attitude* toward life. You're tuned into the same wavelength, and until the circuit blows a fuse (as it might through life's circumstances), you follow the electricity of each other's thoughts. Basically, a True-Blue Friend supplies whatever you consider fun is, whether it be a stimulating, meaningful conversation, shared interests or a lot of laughs.

Other adjectives describe this quality of true-blueness. Can you match any of them to your current special friends?

understanding	warm
forgiving	patient
mind reader	accepting
stimulating	relaxing
helpful	thoughtful

Do any of your friends have these or similar True-Blue qualities? Do any friends you think are True-Blue *not* have them?

Are any friends as True-Blue as the ancient legend of Damon and Pythias? Damon offered his own life as a pledge for his friend, Pythias, when he was condemned to death for rebelling against the king. The pledge enabled Pythias to return to his hometown to get his affairs in order and say good-bye to his family while Damon took his place. As the execution date loomed, Pythias did not return. The king taunted his loyal friend, telling Damon he was a fool to think friendship could ever be so great that one person would forgo the opportunity to save his own neck. The king told Damon that if he had a true understanding of the ways of human nature, he would know that Pythias had surely escaped by now and was far away. On the day of execution, as Damon was being led out to die, Pythias arrived. He ran up trembling, breathless, explaining that an unexpected delay had caused him to arrive late. He was afraid he was too late. Affectionately, the friends greeted each other for the last time and said their final farewells. The king, however, was so deeply moved by this friendship, he pardoned Pythias. With an envious note in his voice, he said, "I would gladly give up my kingdom to have such a friendship as this."

Most of us don't have friends who would give their lives so that we might live, but we aren't likely to put them to that test. The main test of True-Blue Friendship is less dramatic and implies merely truth. If you wonder if a person is a True-Blue Friend, try this exercise:

Go now in your mind's eye to a time and place and ask yourself whether you were honest and real with that person at that time. Don't think, just go. It will come into your mind.

If you were not, this is not the moment to castigate yourself but rather to use that knowledge to extend yourself in true friendship now.

If you were real and honest, you do have a True-Blue Friend. But not every friend will be this "treasure." Some won't even be gems. Still, all belong in your life. To learn to tell the True from the "Not-So-True," let's begin by recognizing the different types of friends.

Historical Friends

Friends you share a history with but don't necessarily share day-to-day experiences with anymore.

"God, Bill and I go back to the fourth grade. We grew up on the same block. Even when we went to different colleges we still remained friends and shared an apartment in San Francisco one year. We were best man at each other's weddings. Then, I settled in Maine and he stayed in California. Now, we see each other every few years. We sure do reminisce about old times, though. But my good friends are those I see day to day." George, accountant, aged thirty-seven.

Historical Friends people the past. They might live across town or across the country. They come back into our lives every once in a while. Then the memories flash as quickly and clearly as slides on a movie projector. The private jokes you remember continue to break you up, though they might bore or puzzle anyone else present. It's a Nostalgia Trip to honor the times you shared, the people you were. Almost everyone has Historical Friends who are threads in the fabric of life.

But not everyone is aware of some of the games we

might play when we meet. Have you ever remarked, "Gee, Freddie hasn't changed a bit since he stole the statue of George Washington for a frat house stunt"? Same old Freddie, a load of laughs. But common sense tells us Freddie must have changed. For one thing, he's many years older and it's a rare person who escapes change with age. For another, he married later than everyone else and then lost his wife to a serious illness. Freddie *must* have changed. But when you see him, he becomes the same good-old-anything-for-a-laugh Freddie. He might come away wondering, "Now, why did I act that way? That isn't me anymore!"

Linda, a seventeen-year-old high school student, was in with a crowd she felt she had outgrown. One summer she went to Europe with some friends on an organized tour. She changed, she thought. She outgrew her friends back home and made a definite decision to try to blend into a crowd that was more appropriate. But when she came home, she found herself in the same crowd, and it took many months before she was able to stop playing the roles everyone expected of her and go on to new friends.

As Historical Friends, we sometimes find ourselves slipping unconsciously into roles we thought we had shed. Sometimes we don't even know it's happening. When you feel yourself sliding into that old role, and you would rather not, create a picture in your mind of your most wonderful adult success, and while you are talking to your Historical Friend, just keep that shining image right in front of you.

We can't minimize Historical Friends, to be sure. They are like living scrapbooks of our past. But they are part of our history and may not work for us in our everyday lives now.

Bar Buddies

A perfect stranger might become a friend for a while over a drink.

"I love to sit at a bar somewhere and booze. The hours seem to pass and everybody's my friend. We talk small talk, sometimes it's more. Nobody holds back because everyone's kind of drunk." Vivian, bookkeeper, age thirty-two.

Alcohol, like marijuana, is a great "open-upper." In bars that promote camaraderie, there is a sense of time standing still. I know one little neighborhood dive where the Christmas lights are up all year round.

People don't go to bars just to drink. Heavy drinkers can belt it down at home or alone if they are dedicated or even problem drinkers. Nowadays, men and women, especially those who live alone, hang out in favorite bars for the comradeship. And sometimes for the bartender, if he's the right kind of grass-roots psychologist. A bar can be an extension of your living room.

Certainly loneliness has a way of attracting Bar Buddies. But bars are not just ghettoes for lonely people. They are also places to form friendships—for a few hours, for one night a week or sometimes to last outside the bar. What you are unable to share with a wife, lover, husband or boss, you might find yourself sharing with a stranger, over a few drinks.

There are single-oriented bars, game bars (darts, pinball machines) and, of course, the singing bars where everyone joins in for a chorus of everything from "As Time Goes By" to an aria from *Aida*.

Once upon a time bars were stigmatized as havens for the lonely, homes for drunkards or pick-up places. Now bars are playrooms for companionship. And women are as at home in them as men. The bar scene fills many a gap in some people's lives and Bar Buddies are fine as friends as long as you don't always need a drink in your hand to reach out and be open.

Your Ex-Lover

You were lovers once, and it seemed right, and now you're not lovers but you've stayed friends and that feels right, now.

"Many of my friends seem surprised that I am still friendly with an old lover. The love affair dwindled, but the friendship is still there. We have no reason not to be friends, we always had a lot in common." Max, college professor, age forty-two.

In Chapter IV, we go into friendships between ex-lovers at great length. Of course, not all ex-lovers stay friends, and many believe it impossible. But it can happen, and when it does, your ex-lover is a kind of Platonic, True-Blue, Convenience Chum, Historical Friend (in a sense) and even Bar Buddy all rolled into one. The next time a love affair sours, if you try to keep the friendship, you may find a very rewarding one, indeed.

Dumpers

Dumpers unload a truckload of misery on you—basically, ordinary problems they can't cope with. They use you. Time and again.

"She used to call me up and launch into her usual tale of woe. One day she called and said, first, 'How are you?' I said, 'I died yesterday.' She went right on to talk about all her problems. She hadn't even heard me." Helen, housewife, age fifty-one.

There's a great difference between a friend who has a legitimate problem to share with you and the Dumper. With Dumpers you get the feeling you're just another ear. If they had a better ear, or anyone equally convenient, they'd use that. They don't expect any feedback. All they demand is that you listen and sympathize with the unfairness of the terrible plight life has just inflicted on them—which usually isn't *that* terrible. When you hang up, or leave, they will go on to the next person and complain about the same thing, or else, unloaded, forget about it (sometimes completely) while you are wearing their problems like a badge. Unless you wise up to Dumpers, they can drag you, unmercifully, down into the depths with them.

One Dumper, who supposedly had the benefit of regular psychotherapy, would hit a slump, call her friends, and let them know just how depressed she was, how nothing was working for her, how life had issued her a bad deal. Dumpers' problems seem unsurmountable. And no wonder they can't be solved; they aren't meant to be solved.

A category of Dumper is the High-and-Low Dumper. High as a kite for one week, this Dumper is really enjoyable company. But then, when things aren't going perfectly, crash! it's down in the dumps again. You might feel you're on a seesaw until you get the hang of it. High-and-Low Dumpers are fair game for life's littlest hurdle. Just when you think they're off and running, they almost always find a way to trip up. And when they do, the gloom they crave is resumed. They have been known to create a problem unconsciously because they worry it will happen!

Remember, it's hard to reform a Dumper . . . and why should you try! Other more stimulating friendships in your life should prove to you that you can do without the

Dumper, who is the type of friend who may not be a friend at all. Can you also tell your Dumper your problem? Does your Dumper depress you? You might wish to dump a Dumper and reclassify him or her as a Former Friend. Unless you enjoy being dumped on. Some people do.

Platonic Friends

A friendship between a man and a woman that is spiritual and intellectual and without sex is platonic.

"I can unwind with Elaine. I'm not especially attracted to her and it's no blow to my male ego that she's not especially attracted to me. She has a fine mind and is really a warm person. At first we were friendly over work we had in common; now we're just friends." Irwin, journalist, age forty-eight.

If you have a Platonic Friend in your life, he or she is quite obviously identifiable. It's when we seek potential friends that we sometimes overlook the vast rewards of Platonic Friendships.

In *The Challenge of Being Single,* authors Marie Edwards and Eleanor Hoover, whose book evolved out of their workshop groups, state that Platonic Friendships do work and should be cultivated.

Surely, we've come a long way from the rigid sexual stereotypes and role-playing of years ago. Woman as sex object and man as pursuer and predator are, frankly, old hat. Both men and women want to be seen as people. And seeing men and women as people first can help the development of platonic friendships.

Yes, you may be thinking, but what if sex enters the picture? That, of course, is the end of the platonic relationship, especially if one person suddenly becomes romantic and the feeling isn't mutual. In fact, there goes the friendship, in many cases.

Not necessarily. And not always. And certainly this caution shouldn't stop you from widening your friendship horizons to include members of the opposite sex. What do you do when your Platonic Friend—or you—suddenly turns romantic? The main thing to remember is you are friends, not lovers. If one of you suddenly wants sex, discuss it, handle it—openly. A young single woman I know was very good friends with a man with whom she had a lot of things in common. The subject of sex never came up. Then he changed, began to ask her "out," and she knew she was in danger of losing their platonic relationship. He called her up and treated her like a *date*. She said, simply, without a lot of explanation, "No, thank you." But the tone in her voice also said, "Don't ever put me in that role again if you want to stay friends." You can also talk to your platonic friend calmly, and tell the truth about your feelings. Sometimes he or she is having a bad time romantically and is reaching out, without realizing it, to the nearest person of the opposite sex.

Platonic Friendships can work. But, like any other friendship, you are free to reject it if it doesn't. The possibility that the subject of sex might arise is certainly no reason not to go after the very rich potentials in a platonic friendship.

Office Friends

Not a True-Blue Friendship, because business often gets in the way of honesty, but a comforting friendship nevertheless.

"I maintain a low profile in the office. There's a great deal of work I have to do and I loathe office politics to the extent I would close my door on it. But, I think, with the pressures that come up during the day, I would not be able to work effectively if there weren't a few people I didn't feel friendly enough with to crack some jokes, talk about things, as well as discuss work-related problems. Also, it's nice to have lunch with someone from the office every once in a while. It's pleasant for work, but that's as far as it goes." Liane, advertising copywriter, age twenty-seven.

There's no how-to manual for forming Office Friend-ships. In many cases, they're better off not formed too tightly. Establishing a True-Blue Friendship with a co-worker has potential built-in disasters, the business world being what it is. Playing the game of survival is the norm here.

The office creates a form of friendship that harmlessly relieves the routine. The mock insults, the jokes, the end-less chitchat. Some people talk about their family, the house they are trying to buy, the dog that was lost and then found. These topics are acceptable to bring to the office. They help ease the workload; they provide homey conversation away from home. Everyone politely cares for just a moment that your daughter's engagement has been broken off or that you need expensive root canal work, then they go home and worry about their own prob-lems or talk to their True-Blue Friends.

Business Acquaintances

Dale Carnegie told his students to enter the office of a person they wanted to impress in business thinking, "I love him. I must smile and talk about his interests, make him feel important, and, above all, not argue with him. He is my friend."

Is he, or she, really? A certain type of friendship, usu-ally not a True-Blue one, does develop between Business

Acquaintances. There is in the business lunches, the business drinks and the business transaction itself a kind of sharing. Sometimes the exchanges involve money, sometimes just a return of a favor or a thank-you gift.

A friend of mine, a therapist, was giving his garage mechanic free therapy for his marital problems. Inevitably, though, the therapist realized he was always late for his next appointment because of this. He decided, why not be honest? "Look," he finally said to the mechanic, "let's have a fair exchange." So the mechanic repaired his car for free while the therapist listened to his marital problems for free.

Are any of your friends really Business Acquaintances rather than True-Blue Friends? Sometimes there is a fine, fine line between the two. The fine line is quite simply: Can you be your true self without a veneer and can the other respond in the same honest vein?

Pygmalion Pals

Pygmalion Pals are great pep-talkers as they tell you what you should do to change your life for what they see must be for the better.

"I had a friend who would interrupt everything I would say with: You should do this or that. Or, it would be a long speech, like 'You must be crazy. You shouldn't quit a job like that. What you need . . .' I really got tired of it. She is a former friend now." Livvy, secretary, age twenty-five.

Pygmalion Pals are sometimes tricky to detect. But their conversation is spiked with such giveaway expressions as "you should . . ." or "you know, what you need is . . ." Their mission in life is to make you over in their image. One Pygmalion Pal might simply say, "You know, what you need is a good conditioner." You are taken off-guard. What's wrong with your hair? Or: "What you should have is a wife—that would solve all your problems. Now, I know a nice girl . . ."

We can all fall into the Pygmalion Pal pitfall if we're not careful. But, what if a friend is actually very overweight, hitting the sauce, throwing a brilliant career down the drain or pining over someone you don't think is half worth it? Do we keep our mouths shut?

Mildred Newman, psychologist and author, with Bernard Berkowitz, of *How to Take Charge of Your Life*, believes people do need friends who speak up instead of ignoring the situation. But it's not *what* you say as much as *how* you say it. The authors feel the most helpful thing a concerned friend can do is to focus on how his or her behavior makes you *feel*. You might say, "You know I consider myself a good friend to you and it just makes me feel terrible to see you gaining weight . . . suffering like that . . . wasting your time with someone who hurts you again and again."

So, there is a difference between making someone with self-destructive behavior patterns listen to what you think and how you feel, and trying to change someone who may or may not have a problem because *you* think it would be better.

Some friends simply have to use their strong parental qualities to try and control your life. If you think this friend is a True-Blue Friend, with maybe this one little blemish, you will feel free to "call" the friend on this bossy aspect of his or her personality. That doesn't mean you do it in a threatening way.

Or, if you like this friend's company, but think it would be difficult or impossible to change the situation, simply limit the time you spend with a Pygmalion Pal. I have a couple of "strong parent" friends I enjoy seeing for their special qualities. But I don't stay with them too long.

The reality is you cannot really change a friend. You cannot help anyone in this world. You can be there, you can listen, you can be warm and caring and love that person. But each of us will do precisely what we want to do in the long run, even though we may say it's because of some advice we got yesterday. We acted on that advice because somewhere lurking in our own consciousness was the desire to hear someone else speak the words we already knew to be true.

If you want to keep a Pygmalion Pal for a friend, don't fight fire with fire, don't try to return a *must* or a *should* or a *you need to*. Fight with the truth, and if you must fight too often, perhaps you would prefer the other person to play Pygmalion Pal to someone else.

Triads

Not two friends, but three friends of opposite and same sexes that form a friendship triangle.

"I'm sharing an apartment with friends of mine. We're roommates. They're a married couple and we all get along fine. We never get in each other's way and are good friends." Bonny, lab technician, age twenty-three.

An embryo of the family networks we will come to, the Triad consists of two people of the same sex and one of the opposite, who, in a threesome, make up a friendship.

Parent-Child Triad

The child, or pseudo-child, may have been brought into the family as a friend of either the man or woman.

The "mother" and "father" are a couple (usually married) who enjoy being with certain single people.

Jack and Brian have known each other for twenty years (no, a pseudo-child doesn't have to be young). Jack went through a painful divorce. When he was married, they were coupled friends. Now he has become the pseudo-child of his friend Brian and Brian's wife, Antoinette. He goes to dinner at their house. Antoinette fusses over him. There are cocktails, his favorite dishes, liqueurs later. All this cushioned by soft music and supportive conversation. This couple is *concerned* about how he is getting along and they enjoy hearing about his single-again adventures. Jack becomes the child; Brian and Antoinette play the parents. No matter, the Triad contains all the elements of friendship. It couldn't exist without a common bond, a shared wavelength and easy conversation.

Ménage à Trois

A trio of singles live together. They don't sleep together, just share the rooms. It may be two men and a woman or two women and a man. This kind of arrangement is usually successful and allows the people to live well, splitting the rent three ways, and not be alone. The hit TV show *Three's Company* is a perfect example of this type of arrangement.

Two women often want "a man around the house." A man may like all the comforts of family life while still retaining his easy status of singleness. Several people who have lived like this have told me that there's a lot of friendly flirtation but no sexual contact. That would destroy the family feeling. "It would be like incest," one said. Thus, there are never any jealousies if one of the Triad dates. It's all brother and sister. It works best when household chores are pooled. The secret of the successful Ménage à Trois is not asking too much from one person, but rather asking less from two. If one member of the trio should let the others down, no one is too disappointed. For people who want to "live together" this is a comfortable alternative to romantic pairing minus the burden of dependency. A lot of honest "family sharing" goes on in the Ménage à Trois.

Friends of Friends

You meet and become friends with the friend of a friend.

"Cynthia was my friend. She threw a party and I met another friend of hers. We are now very close friends." Jacqui, occupational therapist, age thirty-nine.

If you are looking for new friendships, you might draw on this ready-made source. The special qualities that attracted you to your friend might also draw you to your friend's friends. Of course, the opposite might be true. You might not be able to stand them.

One good thing about meeting friends of a friend is that you may have heard about them already. The cliché, "Oh, I've heard so much about you," actually becomes very true. You almost know each other before you meet.

You might make friends by being part of a family unit. Your child's friend's parents become your friends and you all go on family cookouts. Your husband's friend's girlfriend becomes your friend. When you can communicate with them alone, without the company of other friends or your social group, they become your real friends.

I must caution you, though, in picking friends of friends to be sensitive about jealousies. Even the cautioning seems silly to me, because I don't associate jealousy with friendship. To me, jealousy means possession. And you cannot possess your friends. But it does sometimes happen that you strike up a friendship with your friend's friend and become . . . friendly. Perhaps more friendly than you are with your original friend, who feels left out and envious. It can get sticky. Do reassure your original friend of the importance of your friendship. Make it clear that it doesn't change things now that you have a new friend, even though that friend was his or her friend first.

Jewish Mothers

A Jewish Mother Friend wants to give, give, give, asking nothing in return and making you feel guilty when that's what she or he gets.

"I had a Jewish Mother friend. He was Italian and definitely not gay, either. A group of us shared a coed beachhouse during weekends one summer. He emerged as the Organizer. There was Louie, breading the chicken, starting the grill, mixing everyone drinks. But every so often he would go off in a huff. No one could jolly him out of these bad moods and we all felt terribly guilty about it. I realize now he was acting like the Jewish Mother, who had given and given and not got back. Behind his back, we even called him 'mother.' " Camille, teacher, aged thirty-one.

The Jewish Mother doesn't have to be Jewish. Any background can qualify. This type of friend can be a woman, man, parent or not. These people have a need to give, because they have a need to be needed.

Kay told me about needing an unusual-shaped container, rather large, to carry a half-prepared recipe to someone's house for dinner on Christmas Day. She started to borrow it from a neighbor but bumped into a woman who lived two blocks away. Kay had long ago nominated her Volunteer-to-the-World. She headed every committee in the neighborhood, organized every charity fund raising and was known by people for blocks around. Kay knew her for a Jewish Mother. When they stopped for a chat and this woman discovered her need she offered to get in her car, drive five miles and get the pot Kay needed, which was in her office from a Christmas party she had organized. Kay refused. She just couldn't add herself to the list of people who had made possible this woman's personal martyrdom.

The Jewish Mother never gives unless he or she really wants to. It's nice to give other people the opportunity to serve us. If the Jewish Mother gives and then makes you feel guilty, remember nobody *makes* anybody do anything. That includes giving. So enjoy it!

Long-Distance Friends

Like Historical Friends, you don't see them very often, but when you do, they are very much friends in your life right now!

"About once a year I make a business trip to London. I have a friend there and we always get together. It seems we just start up where we left off the last time." Edward, banker, age thirty-seven.

With crisscrossed lifestyles, you may get to see or talk to Long-Distance Friends only once in a while. Yet they may be some of your very closest friends. I think Confucius sums it up in a nice way:

> *Life leads the thoughtful man on a path of many*
> *windings.*
> *Now the course is checked, now it runs straight again.*

Here winged thoughts may pour freely forth in words,
There the heavy burden of knowledge must be shut away
  in silence.
But when two people are at one in their inmost hearts,
They shatter even the strength of iron or of bronze.
And when two people understand each other in their
  inmost hearts,
Their words are sweet and strong, like the fragrance of
  orchids.

—"Fellowship with Men," *The I Ching*

I have a very dear Long-Distance Friend, Eleanor. She lives in California. I phone her long-distance from wherever I am. Four friends, including me, have access to her home when she is away. We all know where the key is hidden. When I'm in California and have a restless day when I know I'm not writing well, I can go there unannounced. Sometimes she's there, sometimes I find the other three, sometimes no one. But it is a true comfort to have a home-away-from-home, to know a good friend lives there. I also know I am completely trusted in the friendship. That became my wedge of feeling at home in California when I lived in hotels. It was the base of a brand new life where I was able to make many new friends and it gave me a sense of belonging. I may not see Eleanor for long periods of time, but she is truly a friend.

Gay and Straight Friends

A heterosexual who is friends with a homosexual or vice versa.
"I have a male homosexual friend. It is absolutely wonderful. Obviously sex never intrudes on our friendship,

yet he has a male point of view, which I welcome! He'll tell me when he thinks I'm being so very female in my attitudes. It's a very supportive friendship for both of us." Alice, public relations executive, age forty.

In the glamorous spots of the world where the Beautiful People congregate, it is a well-known fact that many of the women are being escorted by homosexual men. One woman, a movie star, still famous yet no longer always working, told me, "I don't like going to a party alone and I prefer to sleep in my own bed later—alone. Don is a marvelous companion, witty and attentive and, of course, there is always that masculine strength there—anyone who denies that homosexual men have that is just not being truthful."

Since many men feel uncomfortable having a close male friend who is heterosexual, I can imagine how threatening it would be to have a gay friend. Some heterosexual women, too, shy away from friendships with lesbians. Here, as well, are the same fears and traditional hangups about getting too close. But we limit our friendship horizons with this kind of thinking.

A lesbian I interviewed was indignant at the suspicion that she would present a sexual threat to another woman in a friendship. "You know, we are not turned on to every woman," she fumed. "How presumptuous people are! Gay people are not necessarily promiscuous. So, it doesn't mean if I become friends with a straight woman, I will be hot for her body. Besides—who says she's got such a hot body!" I laughed. She was so right.

What are the rewards of having homosexual friends or—if you're gay—of having straight friends, you might ask? What's in it for you? Why not stick to your own kind? But it's the person we are considering. The main question is the same one that comes up in any discussion of friendship: Can the *person* be a friend?

Convenience Chums

They pop up in your life at a most convenient time and the friendship is based on the fact that they are in your life at that time.

"I met Marty at this party and we became friendly. Then every weekend we would go around together to singles dances and bars looking for girls. Then, one night, he 'lucked out' and met this very nice girl he married within a few months. Now, I'm still friendly with him and his wife has invited me to dinner a few times, but it's just not the same friendship it was." Gus, computer programmer, age thirty.

These friends weave in and out of our lives. We may lose them to time and circumstances, or they may develop into deeper friends who can last a lifetime. A Convenience Chum can be a next-door neighbor, a roommate in college, the mother of little Jody who helps you serve cookies and milk every Wednesday at the local nursery school, the father who drives all the kids on the block to Sunday School or the classmate at night school who doesn't mind helping you with your logic homework.

They are, in a word, convenient. And that is why they are in your life at the time. The convenience is the basis of your friendship. But, unlike other friends, though we may see them even daily, we observe unwritten boundaries (at least until they develop into closer friends, which they may never do). For instance, we may commiserate with them about inflation and enjoy the conversation while we decorate the gym for our kids' high school dance, but we would never dream of telling them we have just remortgaged the house and are in hock up to our necks.

If the timing is right, if your lifestyles merge, and if the chemistry is perfectly blended, the Convenience Chum can become a True-Blue Friend.

This sometimes happens to mothers of young children. I remember it happened to me. Several of us found our lives were remarkably similar. We talked about vaporizers and traded clothes for our children and sympathized on such earthshaking subjects as Dickie outgrowing yet another pair of shoes and the "baby" dumping cereal all over his or her hair. Each of my friends, at that time, could have served duty in another's house so alike were our lives and our ways of handling them. I don't know where they are now, most of these women. Sometimes I walk by a playground and remember how we all were, the young mamas. But I doubt now that any of us would have as much in common as we did then, when it was convenient to be friends.

Do you have any Convenience Chums in your life now? Do they have potential to grow into something more? Or, after analyzing your friendship, would you rather they didn't? Sometimes the timing with which friends enter our life is so important it can overshadow the quality of the friendship, for a while.

The Old and the Young

Crossing the generations and reaching out in friendship to someone much older than or younger than you.

"There was a marvelous old woman who lived across the hall from me in one apartment. She was eighty-six and lived alone. She had lived it all and I loved listening to her stories and telling her about mine. Age was no barrier; she was more modern in her thinking than some of my contemporaries. I could only become friends, speak openly, when I dumped my respectful image of her as a grandmother substitute. She wanted to be a friend, too."
Jocelyn, buyer, age twenty-six.

"I have a friend. On a nice Saturday afternoon, we play basketball in the park near where we live. I've learned a lot from him. He's ten." Michael, attorney, age thirty-five.

Though we feel comfortable with our contemporaries, one of the most interesting and rewarding experiences is to reach across the generations and find—there is no gap. Friends can come in all sizes, types, colors and ages.

A young man lives in a bachelor apartment and rents from a seventy-year-old Latvian refugee. This is a man who always has a bottle of milk in his refrigerator Kevin can borrow when he hasn't had time to shop. This man entertains him with stories of his colorful life in Latvia and attempts at finding his way in America. Kevin, who is adept at fixing anything that vaguely ticks, helps him maintain the apartment and does any heavy lifting for him.

A young woman lives alone. She doesn't yet know if she wants to get married and she almost certainly doesn't think she wants to interrupt her career for children. But she loves kids. So, she adopts a friend's child, whom she likes. They go to movies, out to lunch, and just talk. The little girl's busy mother is happy her daughter has such a friendship in her life. So is the little girl.

If a potential friend from across the generations crosses your path, don't dismiss the relationship as being out of sync. The old and the young have a very special way of rounding out our friendship circle.

Special-Interest Friends

The friend with whom you share a special interest, activity, or ideology.

"I have a friend I like to go to dance concerts with. None of my other friends seems to like modern dance, but we do. Then we usually go out to eat afterward and talk about it. That's our friendship." Ann, artist, age twenty-four.

Sometimes these friends are called Activity Friends because the friendship is based on the activities we share with them. I prefer the name Special-Interest Friends, because often you don't just share an activity, such as basketball or tennis, but rather a philosophy or professional interests. Special-Interest Friends may be your nearest, dearest friends—or you may never be really intimate at all.

You can have many Special-Interest Friends, as different as your interests are. One for clothes shopping, one for playing a sport, one for taking a course with. The friendship you have is based on *doing*, for the most part, instead of just *being* with the person. Special-Interest Friends come and go. A true test of whether that person could ever become a True-Blue Friend is: If you give up playing racquetball on Wednesday nights, would he or she still want to get together with you?

Summer Friends and Traveling Companions can also be Special-Interest Friends. It's a well-known fact that most summer friends you shared your outdoor grill and heart and soul with in the country, you wouldn't travel crosstown to get together with in the dead of winter. Travel experts say, too, that sometimes best friends do not make the best bedfellows when it comes to traveling. You might look for a Traveling Companion who complements you, wants the same travel routine, has the same amount of money to spend, lets you have your privacy occasionally. Someone who shares travel as a special interest might be a better bet for traveling than a close friend.

Fairweather Friends

When your life gets a little stormy you may find friends who want friendship only as long as there are sunny skies.

"When my husband was living, we had a summer home. All our coupled friends would drive out. Then he passed away and I find all those good friends have disappeared. I, of course, am not part of a couple anymore. At first I was lonely, hurt, left out—all those things. But I've made other friends now who are really good friends." Molly, part-time receptionist, age sixty-two.

Though some of the friends discussed in this chapter may be relatively new to you, certainly Fairweather Friends are not. We all have had some experience with this type of friend. But most people know Fairweather Friends in retrospect; they realize what they are too late.

How can you spot the Fairweather Friend before the storm? Beyond having a crystal ball or impeccably astute judgment of character, you really can't. You can observe, though, someone you think is Fairweathering another friend. Did one of your friends break his or her leg and land in the hospital? Did a supposedly good friend fail to visit or call that person? A good way also might be to assess how well a friend responds to real feelings—sorrow, death, anger, any life situation that requires depth.

Not all your friends have to be super-supportive. Fairweather Friends are fun for fair weather. And that's fine, as long as you don't expect more from them.

The opposite of Fairweather Friend turned up in a cover article in *Time* magazine (July 3, 1978). It was about Warren Beatty, movie star and filmmaker. He was referred to by his friend Lillian Hellman as "a foul weather friend." Or, "the first person to call in a crisis." Though it would be quite natural to think of this type of friend as a True-Blue Friend, that isn't necessarily accurate. Some friends come naturally to our aid only during times of personal disasters—then they go on their way. They may be a rarer breed than the Fairweather Friend, but they do exist.

You may even have more kinds of friends in your life! All these categories help us to get clear on the True and "Not-So-True" Friendships! And there are more.

Chapter IV
Man-to-Man, Woman-to-Woman, Black and White, Lovers and Ex-Lovers, Other Couples and Other-Than-Coupled Friendships.

"What is a friend? A single soul dwelling in two bodies."
—Aristotle

I know that my closest friendships have always been with women. I can share my innermost thoughts and know in my gut that the woman friend will truly understand the delicate nuances of my deepest feelings. Because we as women are accustomed to sharing who we are, the good and the bad of it, we tap into that deep reservoir where the life forces exist.

Am I saying that men are unable to do this? Of course not. And yet it is so difficult for many of them. It is even harder for many women to have a friendship with a man without sex lurking as the basis for the relationship.

I am fortunate; I do have male friends. We do share the intimacies of our lives, and in order to get to that point, we had to openly and honestly discuss sex, and go through that barrier, before we could be simply friends.

I am reminded of that now clichéd cartoon. Are you familiar with it? The one that shows a little girl and little boy holding out their pants and looking down, exclaiming, "Hey, they're different!" I think soon after little girls and boys make the initial discovery that there *is* a difference, they play more closely with friends of their own sex. Eventually, the motto becomes: No sex, no games.

This is truly a remarkable time to form new friendships because so many of the notions we used to have about what is right and proper are rapidly disappearing. And yet in an era of transition the old dies hard as men cling to their macho way of having friends not only to exclude women but also to feel comfortable themselves.

Man-to-Man

Men do inhabit a special world that women never quite penetrate, though some may think they do. Even in a bar where a woman is sitting with her feet on the barstool, I have heard a man say, "Watch your language, there's a lady present." I have also been in meetings, business meetings, where, as the only woman, I have seen a man turn to another man with the punch line of a dirty joke so a woman couldn't hear. Old-fashioned? Yes, but behavior that goes back a long, long way. In primitive times, men did the hunting, the fishing, and the fighting while womenfolk tended the fires and took care of the children. Even if, perhaps, women did more than comb lice out of each other's hair, watch each other's kids and cook what the menfolk clubbed, men, physically stronger, were the ones to venture outside the cave or hut. Men probably reasoned that it would be better to group together in bands for safety. And today that safety includes banding together against the power of the woman, especially since women have become more open about using their power. I think that many men seek their private male refuges against the increasing and insistent power of women who may pose a threat far greater than that posed by animals in the wild.

Henry Higgins summed it up best in *My Fair Lady*, when he lamented to his good friend, Colonel Pickering, "Why can't a woman be more like a man?"

All-Male Clubs

Anthropologist Robert Brain reiterates the fact that men simply feel more at ease in the company of other men, with women excluded. In locker rooms, where men are traditionally permitted to show genuine physical affection for one another, swatting of towels, bear hugs after a successful game, a lot of good-natured pushing, shoving, screaming, and champagne shampoos pass for intimacy. These are the ways in which it is acceptable for one man to say to another, "Hey, I really like you," and hide all those scary latent homosexual feelings. Traditionally, women have not suffered the same stigmas. We can kiss and hug without being labeled lesbians. (I am not putting any stigma on lesbians, I am simply reporting the way "society" feels.) Yet, let a man openly hug another man and he is suspect.

So when men are in their all-male sanctuary of locker room or club or fishing excursion, they are safe as long as they express their love for one another in a jovial way. And they feel safer and more at home with one another when the critical eye of woman is not looking at them. Women represent the once-powerful mother instructing the man to do something, to "clean your fingernails," "keep your room neat." Women are a reminder to heterosexual men that they have to perform sexually. With all these shoulds lurking in the back of men's minds it's no wonder that they find it a lot more relaxing to simply swat a towel, tell a dirty joke, laugh, and relax. No admonitions, no expectations. Only recently are some men willing to look at themselves and their friendships.

Beyond Macho

The 1960s brought about the cultural shift. When men decided that their hair could be long, that they didn't have to fight in a war that some considered immoral, that it was fine to wear love beads and chains around their necks—these were the signs that they were no longer willing to be the stereotyped macho male. Some men, of course, will always feel safer in the old roles. But some are willing to risk new ones.

In the February 1978 issue of *Esquire* magazine, author John Gregory Dunne writes of his friendship with another author, Josh Greenfield. I discuss their relationship here not to make fun of what Mr. Dunne feels friendship is, but because I was amazed.

Mr. Dunne writes that he and his good friend Josh Greenfield talk as often as four times a day on the telephone. They say they are the "best of friends." Yet, Dunne announces almost immediately, he has never been inside his good friend's home in all the years they have known each other. Why? Because Josh Greenfield has a brain-damaged son, Noah. Dunne writes that the two friends do a lot of laughing and joking around and lunching together, but *never* at Josh Greenfield's home.

I am surprised; I find this remarkable. I simply cannot imagine two women being dear friends, one having a brain-damaged child, and the other woman *never* going to the home, *never* interacting with the child. And never even talking about it! It is inconceivable to me to call that friendship.

Then Dunne explains why he prefers not to get involved in that side of his good friend's life: "We rarely admit how many filters there are on even the closest friendship. We filter what we tell our friends, we filter what we receive from them. The quicksand of our own lives is so treacherous that friendship, at times, seems an almost fatal freight."

He feels there is a "certain calm to be found in the lives of strangers."

I cannot imagine a woman expressing herself that way. There are relationships in my life in which I have "removed all filters." I find it sad that many men conduct their relationships with filters. Their affection cannot be openly expressed, and for that they truly suffer. Their affection is expressed in the joking around; their deepest feelings, never.

I do not fault the author, I merely see him and others like him as the product of our societal conditioning for the male. Like the women who cannot recognize the assertive part of their natures, some men choose not to deal with their emotional side. And when they do, it is haltingly, or under the influence of a few extra drinks, or in the darkness of the night. I certainly don't deny the deep supportive relationship of two men who talk four times a day on the telephone, but I find it impossible to see myself in a situation where the retarded son of a close friend is not a fit topic for discussion, nor visiting the home part of the friendship. Since Josh Greenfield's boy, Noah, has been the subject of a best-selling book by his father, his existence is certainly not a secret.

Thank the beginnings of men's liberation that not all men feel the way Dunne does.

The once-forbidden side of a man's nature, the gentler, softer side, has been given permission to emerge in the 1970s. And some men are delighted with the new image of their sex and only too happy to share less macho aspects.

Because homosexuality is far more widely accepted than it ever has been in our society, the fear of it, which helped to keep men's friendships stiff and superficial, is gradually disappearing. The suspicion that a man is homosexual if he cries or discloses his gentle nature is not quite the threat it once was.

It's Okay for Men to Hug Now

Yes, I know staunchly heterosexual men who will walk up to one another and hug. I know heterosexual men who will openly acknowledge male friendship with kissing. I know heterosexual men who are not afraid to cry in front of one another.

The heterosexual male is saying "Yes, I have this homosexual part of my nature which I may or may not express sexually in real life, but it's perfectly okay to express part of it in friendship with another man."

Jack Schwartz, a psychologist, feels that "manliness is killing men." He told me that "it is even unmanly for a man to fail at suicide." (And while more women try to commit suicide, more men succeed. That is what the statistics tell us.)

All of us have two aspects of our nature, the male and the female. When a man swears a lot, you can be pretty sure he is fighting his female side. In many of us these two parts are always warring, but they don't have to be. When a man feels free to let his feelings emerge, he is simply allowing his feminine side to come to the foreground. And conversely, when a woman permits her assertiveness to come out, she is expressing her masculine side.

The essence of most of the recent books on men's liberation is that men have the right to express that submerged part of their personality, the soft, female, yielding aspects. And it truly benefits women. This is the kind of sharing that women long for in their relationships with men.

They not only love it, they need it. The old shoot 'em up cowboy is not the female romantic idol. Far from it. When Clark Gable acted the tough macho male in *Gone With the Wind*, that wasn't the part women kept returning to see; it was the gentleness and tenderness he showed that forty years later make this a memorable male role in a still-timely movie. The feminine side of a man's nature makes him more masculine to women. And most women I know have had it with the swaggering toughness of macho men. They know it isn't real, they know it is only a shield, and when they don't pity it, they hate it.

Men, you can be closer to women; our intimate relationships, our friendships, all will benefit as we drop the roles we thought we were "supposed" to assume. That tough conditioning dies a hard, slow death, especially in men over thirty-five. At least, I have observed that younger men are more ready to be open with their feelings, without feeling they are "less" or "worse" or "weak" or "scared."

Scared is probably the key word here; men have to face their fears in order to enjoy the bond of close friendship with another man or with a woman. The men I see want the same kind of wholeness that many women are achieving. Strangely, I feel it is easier for a woman to express her masculine, assertive side than it is for a man to express his gentle, feminine side. It looks as if the man has more to lose, but once he expresses it, then he has no qualms. He simply knows that it feels good to be completely who he is—a human being. And I have yet to meet a woman who didn't relish the man who has removed the wraps on his emotions. Swaggering toughness belongs to another era, another world where "making it" consisted of fighting everyone and everything. That's not now.

Woman-to-Woman

The women's movement has changed society. Even women who are adamantly against it as the breakup of the nuclear family and a grotesque stretching of woman's nature must agree to one thing—in the last fifteen years, much has changed. More jobs and professions are open to women; they are not just "tokens." Psychologically, women see themselves in a new light. The song "I Am Woman," by Helen Reddy, is as much a banner as the catch phrases Gay Rights and Black is Beautiful. And yet there is plenty of competition among women these days. The difference is, it's no longer hidden and some of it is very different in kind.

The Jealousies

The underlying tension in female friendship is named *jealousy*. It used to be apparent only on one level, competing for the ultimate prize—a man. It doesn't have to be the same man; it could be just "man" in general. In case the cries of protest roar too loud, I beg you to remember these lines (because they might still be heard):

"Sure, I'd love to do something Saturday night, unless I get a date."

"If nothing better comes along [meaning a man], we'll get together."

Silent line: "So, that's what his secretary looks like. She's too attractive."

I had thought we'd gone beyond that kind of old-fashioned competitiveness, placing the man on a priority pedestal, until . . . until one day I found myself calling a woman friend to cancel a movie and dinner date because a man had materialized from California. He was an ex-lover, someone I was no longer fond of, much less in contact with. I thought I accepted because I hadn't seen him for a long time. But I realized he wasn't a good friend anymore. What I was really doing, from old habit, was saying to myself, "The date with the woman doesn't count as much; I have a date with a man. The woman is unimportant; she'll understand."

As soon as I understood what I was doing, I called up my woman friend and explained. It was a good thing, too, because she was angry. Not very many women today will accept second-class status automatically. I could have ruined my relationship with her. I called the man and declined. I said I was busy, after all. But, I wonder, how many women still accept a date with a man, any man, just because he's a man, and break a previous engagement with a good woman friend? Though this was always "understood" in female friendships of the past, I think it just doesn't wash anymore; it doesn't belong in the friendship vocabulary we are acquiring.

Men have accused women of being innately bitchy. Supposedly they will turn on another woman without the slightest provocation. They are catty; they don't trust each other the way men trust each other. Since I know many warm and wonderful women who don't fit this stereotype, I am always mystified by this common picture of females. But I think I do understand what women have been taught for centuries: Man defines you. We must catch a man, "snare" him, and manage to keep him even when our competition is a new crop of nubile beauties almost half our age. Then we have to protect our turf. No wonder women seem always to be sharpening their claws. It is difficult for a woman to act if she has traditionally been programmed to react. And with this set of rules, how can she trust another woman!

This may sound dreadfully passé to those women who feel they have gone beyond all this. But there is a new underlying tension that miscolors some women's friendships, and it is still competition. Not the same competition that prevents men from forming deep, open friendships, but a multifaceted competition that, like an octopus, can strangle the "sisterhood" women speak of so glowingly.

With the woman's movement, jealousy has boomeranged. Now man may not be the prize, but achievement. On one side is the Traditional Woman who defines her success through her man's. On the other side is the New Woman who is independent, not afraid to be single, career-oriented, who defines herself by her own successes. Both might think they're on solid ground until they meet *each other*, and then the parrying begins. The Traditional Woman feels she's unimportant and the New Woman feels unwanted.

This was spelled out to me, recently, when I met an old friend from "way back when." Lillian had lived the life of glamorous career girl until she married a much older man who takes very good care of her in enviable style. Her talk was filled with patter about her jewelry acquisitions, her luxurious trips to the tropics, her gorgeous wardrobe and, of course, her doting husband. My talk was filled with a forthcoming cross-country tour promoting a book I was terribly excited about, my new projects and a possible brief vacation, when I would stay at a friend's beach house in Hawaii.

Now, I can't remember when I haven't enjoyed my independence and the continuous self-discovery that goes with it. So why was I sitting there pushing my salad around thinking, "Hmm, yes, but she's got a husband. And what a life!"

I couldn't believe my thoughts and I don't know which was worse—the jealousy or admitting I felt that way. Logic argued: "Are you crazy? You have everything you've ever wanted. You're having a ball." Emotion countered: "Yes, I know, but you see, I'm not married. And she is. She has someone. Someone wants her and cares for her." I felt insecure.

I discovered the more I knew this jealousy for exactly what it was, the more it subsided. I kept on top of the lunch by simply acknowledging that the jealousy existed. After a while, I stopped my mental interrogation. The more I felt it for what it was, the more I could put it aside and actually be there at the lunch. Afterward, when we parted, I thought of it again. My eyes cleared and I acknowledged her lifestyle was unattractive to me. She was beautifully taken care of, but in her marriage she was not her own person and had nothing of her own. I can't really say she was blissfully happy, either.

Where had the jealousy stemmed from? From conditioning, yes; I had been sucked in by her "look what I've got, look what kind of man has chosen me, look how he adores me." And the underlying implication was: Maybe your career is fun, but it's not a man. She wanted to dazzle me, because of her own insecurities! I saw, too, how easily this can reverse itself. A woman who has a career can enthusiastically advertise how wonderful her lifestyle is. Had I done that, consciously or unconsciously? Had it been misinterpreted? Had that triggered the competitiveness? I wasn't sure and I'm still not. But I do know she succeeded in making me feel jealous because I let her! I fell right into the old trap of the woman-to-woman Let's

Compete Game, which has been updated for the times we live in.

Competitiveness, as we have seen in male friendships, does not make for the kind of open, feeling communication we hope to achieve in our friendships. I think if women dropped all this and merely reached out to one another, as so many already do, we could put competitiveness on a rocket ship to the moon. Simple logic tells us that a man is neither the prize, nor the booby prize. And there need be no war between lifestyles women have chosen. One doesn't have to defend. A woman can take up an occupation, go to school and still have a husband and children in her life. We do make our own choices. Women's lives are changing and every woman is responsible for living her own life. We should respect that choice and each other.

Are Black and White Friendships Possible?

June, a woman of thirty-four, remembers her childhood in Chicago. "My best friend lived next door. A little black boy about five called Junior. At that age I didn't know the difference between black and white and we were inseparable. I was welcome in his house and he in mine. Then we had to move, because the neighborhood became predominantly black. I wonder if we would have grown up together as friends?"

Many, many neighborhoods have "changed." Blacks are moving out of the inner cities and into traditionally white middle-class suburbs.

I asked Mike, a young black man of twenty-five who lives and works in New York City, what he thought, since he has done a lot of thinking about this subject. He came from Barbados ten years ago, where blacks were the majority, and he's still not accustomed to the separateness. He says it's "an attitude" he can feel. "Most whites look at blacks and stereotype them. I have to wait for acceptance, wait until they get to know me."

Mike feels the history of our country, which includes over a century of slavery, is the cause of the anger and disparity between the races. He feels that the two races have a long way to go if this disparity is ever to be healed.

But he does have white friends. What June said, I heard from him: "It doesn't matter if the person's red, white, or purple. I can't see the difference. I look for the person." He also told me about a white friend who had said to him, "You're my friend and I don't see you as black. I just see you as my friend."

Perhaps the two races do have a "long way to go" on friendship. But one of my very good friends is Moses Gunn, the well-known black actor. I see him as neither black nor white but a person who's a kindred spirit in my life. He's stayed in my home while acting in Philadelphia.

We could probably all learn a lesson from children who can't tell the difference. For the difference is taught to us by people who think they know what it is. Aristotle once said, "What is a friend? A single soul dwelling in two bodies." Souls have no color, only bodies do. Perhaps it will be as individuals that we break the color separation, by reaching out and touching hands in friendship.

Can Lovers *Really* Be Friends?

"Of course," you are thinking, dewy-eyed and idealistic. Real lovers are real friends. Yes, I'm thinking that, too, but why is it so many real lovers reach the altar and part ways soon after, as our soaring divorce statistics prove? Did all of them decide not to be love-mates and part amicably as friends, or were they not really friends to begin with? Or, did love get in the way of friendship until they could no longer communicate? A lot of questions here! Maybe the answer is that getting involved in love covers up our feelings. And that interferes with friend-ship.

One woman explained to me, "When you're young and single, you get this difference confused a lot. There is no difference between your friend and your lover. There is a lot of difference between friends and people you sleep with." I think this same difference could apply to a spouse as well.

It could also apply to homosexual couples. I have two gay friends who live as a couple and their relationship is much like a heterosexual marriage. Good sometimes. The same kinds of games and basic arguments other times. The real problems occur when their friendship breaks down.

Not too long ago a young woman friend came to visit me with the man she planned to marry. They were mov-ing from the East Coast to the West Coast to begin life from scratch. Not easy to do—relocate and start a mar-riage simultaneously.

"Bob is my friend, first," she quickly said, "and that makes it easier. First of all, we've known each other for five years. Our marriage isn't based on some romantic Hollywood notion of love."

"Terrific!" I agreed. "That is, if you can keep this friendship going."

"*If?*" they both chimed in.

"Precisely," I warned them and it was the voice of ex-perience. Not only mine, but others' I knew as well.

"Often, when two people live together every day, the truth gets stuck somewhere inside and the friendship that seemed so easy and natural is one day gone."

They looked at each other. Bob and Janet had lived together for a few years, but they knew it was not the day-after-day sharing of problems a marriage required. I suggested that they would continue to remain friends if they remained *in truth*. Because that's what real friendship is all about. I also cautioned them just how difficult that might be when they lived their lives together.

Angers, frustrations, hurts arise. One person thinks, "Well, I can't discuss *that* with him." Or, "She'll never understand. She'll get angry. She'll be hurt. I can't even find the words to get it out."

And the strong subconscious rule between lovers: "He/she expects me to be happy. I'd better not rock the boat."

In this era of statistic-spinning divorce, I know several lasting (twenty-five year) marriages that work well. *All of the couples attributed the root of their marriage to friendship.*

One woman I talked to, Inez, made her point very clear. "Mark never lets me get away with any of my 'stuff.' I can't pull tricks with him. When he thinks I'm wrong, or covering up my emotions, he tells me. He can sense it. We know each other that well. I do the same with him. And we both listen to what the other person is saying. I tell him right out when I'm angry. But I never blame him."

In my opinion, Inez hit the target with the word *listen*. For lovers are friends when they truly listen to each other. Not justify. Not interrupt. Not defend. Just give their full attention and listen. If lovers truly want to be friends, they must learn to open their eyes and ears for the truth.

When a relationship does break, or begins to come

apart, the truth will often spill out anyway—flying from everywhere in anger. Two normally loving people can suddenly tear each other apart verbally, sometimes physically, and even with silence. The shock of hearing emotions and ideas bottled up for so long can be an ugly surprise. "You never told me you didn't like my doing this!" That person might have been doing it for ten years, but . . . this is the first time she or he heard the truth. Or worse, the explosion happens but the truth never manages to emerge.

I feel the reason so many couples dissolve is that they become "careful" about telling their negative feelings to each other. They won't let them out for fear it will disrupt the relationship. But that is precisely the problem, the stifling of feelings that builds up until there is a final explosion that ends in a bang or a whimper.

I know a woman who had been married to a man for fifteen years. She treated him like a fragile doll rather than a human being. She catered to his every need, wish and comfort, or so she thought. Living up to her image of the wifely role, she was very careful to conceal from him any of the real issues of their marriage. Worries about the children, sexual dissatisfaction, anything at all she considered unpleasant she spared him.

She did tell everyone proudly what a happy marriage they had. Two handsome, bright children; a lovely home in suburbia; her husband's prestigious corporate job— they had the American Dream. Until one day, out of the blue, he came home from work and packed a suitcase. He announced he was leaving. There was no "other woman." He had had enough of Let's Pretend. He had been miserable for years, he admitted. Just like that, the American Dream crumbled into a nightmare.

My friend was totally devastated. Had he lost his mind? Was it midlife crisis? They had everything and he was just throwing it away. She learned later that they had everything in their marriage but the one basic ingredient that would make it endure—friendship. Not only had she never trusted or wanted to look at the truth, she had run away from it. They had no truths with each other. They weren't friends. Her husband's sudden departure wouldn't have been such a surprise if they had been.

Do you have a friendship with a lover or mate? Take this quiz and see just how good a friend you are to each other:

Friends and Lovers Quiz

1. Do you often "slide" over a hurt feeling, not saying anything?

2. Do you let the "real" you come out when you are angry or upset?

3. Do you often tell yourself everything's okay in your relationship, when you know deep down that everything's not all right?

4. Do you have a same-sex best friend you tell the whole truth to—the truth you would never tell him or her?

5. Did you share yourself more honestly at the beginning of your relationship?

6. Do you feel it's frightening or wrong to tell the truth to a lover? Or do you feel that's something for the younger generation?

7. Have you *ever* had an honest relationship with a husband, wife, or lover?

8. Can you be honest without "dumping" on the other person?

9. Can you be compassionate while the other is telling the truth, or are you quick to jump in with "I could have told you so" or "You should have done it that way"?

10. Do you have a glossy relationship that appears idyllic to outsiders but you know, somewhere in your heart, there's something missing?

Obviously, this is not meant to be a trick quiz. You should be able to guess the answers fairly quickly. But, to double-check, here is what you should have answered if you are friends with your lover: 1) No. 2) Yes. 3) No. 4)No. 5) No. 6) No. 7) Yes. 8) Yes. 9) Yes 10) No.

If more than a few of your answers don't agree, you might stop and think—why not? If too many of your answers don't match the desirable answers (most especially the answer to the last question), your friendship and relationship may be destined for trouble. Far from being friends—or enemies, for that matter—you may become strangers and end up feeling lonely together. Better to talk everything out now and communicate as friends. It's a good habit to get into if you want to stay lovers.

Can Ex-Lovers Be Friends?

Perhaps the most touching lovers and ex-lovers to walk across the cinematic screen in the last few years are Diane Keaton and Woody Allen. The movie based on their "loosely autobiographical" story is, of course, *Annie Hall.* In real life they are, as they have attested, ex-lovers but the best of friends.

People can and do remain the best of friends after they are no longer lovers. Ruth, a woman who feels this is nat-

ural, told me, "The ex-lovers I still have as friends are
men with whom I have *cleaned up* the relationship. We
have redefined our relationship. We no longer have a
need to be lovers, but we want to remain friends. I have
to be very truthful with myself about what I still want
from a man if this should happen. To clean up a relationship takes it into a new perspective: The sex is gone, but
you don't want the person to leave your life. I can think of
one where it took years before we could really be friends.
But I think it's wonderful never to lose a friend because
you have ceased to remain in a love relationship. Think of
it—the relationships that turn into friendships are relationships that could last a lifetime."

Sheri, who left New York to go to Michigan with her
new husband, returns every summer, alone, on a separate vacation to stay with an old girlfriend. One July she
got the nerve to phone an ex-lover, whom she had been
curious about and whom she had been engaged to for a
time. As luck would have it, he was in when she called
and he invited her to have coffee with him. Quickly, she
swallowed a tranquilizer and called her girlfriends to put
them on red alert. Was it *just* coffee that she was after?
Would she be attracted to him? Did she have a two-year
marital itch? Would she end up having a brief affair while
her husband was home diapering their baby?

What she found, in the coffee shop, was an attractive
man who couldn't hold a candle to her husband, whom
she now prized even more dearly. She also found a new
friend. And this was the big revelation for Sheri. For
while they had been lovers, they had never been truthful
in the relationship. He was even telling her now of un-
truths in his present love relationship. He had no inten-
tion of ever marrying the woman he was living with,
though she hoped for it. He saw at least one other woman
secretly. When Sheri was going with him, he had sworn

that he had stopped seeing a particular woman—the woman he was living with now! Yes, they had been dating all along. So many lies. But they didn't have to play the game of lovers anymore. Sheri and her "ex" could talk as friends. Sheri remarked later, "My God, I very nearly married him! And we didn't even *know* each other." Love, or what she believed to be love at the time, had clouded Sheri's eyes. Now, friendship opened them. They're free to be friends, free to be truthful.

"Very sweet," a man burdened with heavy alimony and child support payments may scoff, "but I can never be friends with a woman who has drained me dry. My ex-wife has taken everything. You expect me to give her friendship?"

Marriage counselor Dr. Herbert Otto also would put some shadows across this particular area of the radiant field of friendship. "I think it is possible to remain friends," he agrees, "but only if there's a minimal materialistic involvement on both parts. You see, it always comes back to the division of property or money. These areas represent tremendous difficulty for people in marital separations. I have seen it over and over in my experience with marriage counseling."

How *do* people who have been married for years keep the friendship from becoming a money brawl once the marriage is over? One answer came quite by accident. I asked a new friend of mine, as I have asked so many people, what friendship meant to her. "Pleasure in each other's company," came her quick reply. And then to my astonishment: "My ex-husband certainly qualifies for that. He is a good friend."

"Your ex-husband is your friend?" I asked. I had never drawn that response.

"Right. Because I no longer love him, so I no longer have to hate him. Now we can be friends. And I very

much want to because we have three children. I want
them to enjoy both of us without that tug of war on either
side."

It wasn't always this amicable for Brenda and her ex-
husband. She had to work at the friendship. "When we
were first divorced," she recalls, "our relationship was at
zero. I deliberately guided it into some sort of friendship
by staying away from those parts of our relationship that
would frighten him. For example, he thought that because I was making overtures to be friends, it might mean
I was trying to draw him back again. I knew he suspected
I was teasing him, keeping him dangling. I was totally
respectful of his fears and talked about them with him.

"Another thing I did when I was getting the divorce
was to call his two sisters and spell it out as succinctly as I
could. 'I'm not getting divorced from you, only from your
brother.' I happen to like them and always have. 'I would
like us to remain friends,' I told them. And we have.

"There were too many doors in my life I couldn't shut—
his relatives, our mutual relationship with the children,
long-time mutual friends. I needed to be friends with my
ex-husband. And I think the main trick is this: If you don't
fall into a hate bag, after you split, you can fall very easily
into friendship."

But, Brenda revealed, there's friendship and there's
friendship. Her need is to keep the peace. She doesn't
talk with her ex-husband about the men in her life or anything that might cause a heated discussion igniting the
flare-up of old differences. Rather than going to the beds
of strangers, they find sex with each other, occasionally,
rather comfortable. "I mean we were married twenty-five
years. But it's friendly, not serious. And not really the
bond that makes our friendship."

One of the realities men and women who divorce in

hate and anger discover is that the partnership existed in hate and anger, too.

Just recently I saw a satirical review in which the troup presented a quiz show winner with her prize: an authentic hippie, petrified since the Democratic Convention of 1968, long hair, love beads, sunglasses, and a supply of drugs to help maintain him. The audience laughed. But I remembered the very important legacy the hippies, flower children of the sixties generation left us with. Remember it? "Open up," they urged. "Bring all that hidden stuff into the open, reach out and love, man, love." We laugh at them now, but they taught us much. For that's what friendship is about.

Wouldn't we all be taking a giant step in love if we met an old lover and extended the hand of friendship rather than the biting tongue of hate? Or, if when we speak to an ex-spouse, every conversation doesn't trap us in the same unresolved argument and just a tiny seed of friendship is planted. Or replanted. The same seed that used to be there a long time ago. It's a beginning.

Other Couple Friends

When you're a couple on campus, other couple friends are not hard to meet. If you're living together, you blend with single couples or married couples. If you always stay in the same hometown, you can easily move in a circle of couples you've known since childhood. But odds are that in our highly mobile society you will be seeking the friendship of other new couples. How does one couple become friendly with another couple?

Most likely one will have a friend and the other will try to be friendly with the husband or wife. Or, one will bring home friends from his or her professional life. Sometimes through joint activities couples meet couples. This does not bring instant friendship, though, because here, too, is the pitfall of role-playing.

I think too many couples knock themselves out trying to impress another couple instead of just getting to know them in friendship. Have you ever been to one of those stiff, coupled dinner parties where the canapés are delicious, the meal divine, the table set with the best china and crystal, but the hostess is a nervous wreck? The atmosphere is one of strain, admiration for the host and hostess's efforts, but no one really has any fun.

So many couples intertwine friendship with impressing the other couple. "Before the feminist movement woke me up," Alison admits, "I was into this group of coupled friends. We all took turns inviting each other to dinner. We honestly enjoyed each other but it turned into a three-ring circus of trying to outdo each other. One time it was my turn and I got so frazzled, my husband was whipped into such a feverish pitch, that I overestimated the cooking hours per pound on a very expensive roast. A whole table of people were sitting there and I delivered it charred and dried out! I was never so mortified in my life. And I have never done anything like that again. From then on it became pizza or spaghetti or hot dogs."

To be sure, it's a hit-and-miss, trial-and-error affair when couples try to establish friendships with other couples. This is understandable. Because instead of two people trying to become friends, four people are involved. Therefore, the ratio of success shrinks. Perhaps the woman hits it off with the other woman and the men go along. Or vice versa. But every once in a while you hit that perfect couple and all four of you become good friends. The only suggestion I have, if you haven't done it already, is to keep on trying to find the perfect couple; it's a warm and special kind of friendship.

The Importance of Other Friends to a Couple

Because of, perhaps, media propaganda and Hollywood love stories, a man and woman in love are supposed to mean everything to each other. The contrived togetherness Betty Friedan exposed in her book *The Feminine Mystique* is still very much with us. When a couple first meets and love is in the air, one can soil it with an innocent remark like "I don't like to ski" if the other one loves it. And so the winter will find an avid skier on the slopes and a disinterested one struggling along in the interests of love or togetherness, or the fear of separateness and the other person finding a new love.

Werner Erhard in the est training says that a relationship that works is giving someone the space to be what that person is, and what he or she is not. The problem today is often that one partner won't give the other person space.

Space includes separate interests and it also includes having your own friends. The irony here is that if your lover is your best friend, but your only friend, it may be rather difficult to maintain that friendship. Whether it's done out of laziness or love or fear, you are locked together by invisible chains and crammed in a box. Unless you are two very unusual people, neither of you will grow and the friendship, not nourished, will eventually go stale.

It adds variety for couples to have separate friends. I think just one daily trial or tribulation shared with a good friend instead of with each other the moment the door opens at night could save a relationship. I think, also, that the misconception, or myth, that love means meaning everything to each other or it's not true love is at the root of our high divorce statistics. When couples begin to leave behind separate friends or fail to seek new ones, the seed of future trouble is planted.

Anthropologist Robert Brain in his book *Friends and Lovers* writes: "Unfortunately I do not believe that the needs of a man and a woman for love and friendship can be satisfied by one single partnership. There has been an attempt by a certain kind of couple to make marriage a Siamese-twin unit in which all emotional needs are satisfied."

Myron Brenton, in his book *Friendship* also comments on this potentially damaging aspect of togetherness:

> In fact, the traditional fabric of American love and marriage, spun from romantic love, is prone to rips and tears because of competition arising from close outside friendships on the part of either partner. Romantic love is exclusive love, mysterious love, powerful-force love, you-render-me-helpless love, you're the only-one-for-me kind of love. In its ultimate state the romantic lovers' world is seen as being without doors or windows to the outside, for the lovers are everything to each other, my beloved and I, what need do we have for the intimacy of close friendship? Romantic love is possessive love, and possessive love creates what Germaine Greer has called "the symbiosis of mutual dependence in which each is the other's only true friend."

Since we have a certain amount of time for work, and a lot of leisure time left over, I think a love relationship that does not let in the sunlight of separate friendships has to stand so much, so continuously, it is impossible for it to survive. Being so together as to be one person all the time is not healthy, I think.

We all need other friends to talk to. Certain friends become very special. Some have a gift that will enable them to function as friend-therapists. Functioning, perhaps, better for us than professional therapists. If we know how to recognize them.

Chapter V
Using a Friend as a Therapist

"The most I can do for my friend is simply to be his friend."

—Thoreau: *Journal,*
February 7, 1841

If the problem you face is so upsetting you feel you cannot go on without discussing it with someone, you have an alternative to calling up a therapist and making an appointment.

That is, if you have a friend.

You can try a friend as a therapist.

You can see if it works for you.

There are hazards, to be sure. You will want to choose the appropriate friend because anything less might be a disaster. You will want to try to refrain from "dumping" on a friend. Even though you are upset, you should somehow let your friend know the favor will be returned should it be necessary. If your friend finds your problem far too complicated, you might then have to decide to seek professional help.

When to Turn to a Friend

Any therapist will tell you that an automatic part of any type of psychotherapy is simply the release of emotion—anger, sadness, depression. Whatever it is that has you feeling troubled.

In many respects, we live in an artificial culture, and don't even realize we are troubled. In business, we often feel anger, but most of the time we cannot afford to express it, or even recognize it, without jeopardizing a job or a career. Out of habit, learned when we were tiny, we skillfully suppressed our angers so our giant caretakers, Mommy and Daddy, wouldn't get angry themselves and abandon us. There are other angers that leave us helpless. Transportation hangups, bureaucratic hassles, the weather fouling up our plans. And, all the while, life speeds by at an ultra-rapid pace. What happens to all these angers we suppress and repress? They have a fair chance of turning into depression. I even hesitate to use the word *depression*, as it is generally known. Let's just say the grim lows in the normal ups and downs of life might feel a little grimmer one day. Especially if you have no one to confide in or don't know why you feel as you do.

But if your depression is so severe you cannot even get up in the morning, cannot relate to others, cannot laugh or share your troubles—cannot function—then, by all means, see a therapist. Do not rely on a friend. It is much too heavy a burden for a friend to sustain. This would apply, as well, to anxiety or whatever else is troubling you.

If, however, your depression or temporary unhappiness is of the garden-variety type, you can take it to a friend. How do you know when?

Here is a brief checklist. If you can answer yes to *every* question, go to a friend first.

1. You are fully functioning.
2. You know once you have someone to talk to, to listen while you get it all out of your system, you will feel better.
3. You are basically in control of the situation; the confusion results from having kept it in.
4. *You know what's troubling you,* even if you can't express it eloquently. It's not just a vague feeling of helplessness or depression or anxiety.

It is true that well-meaning friends might, at first, try to "jolly" you out of your current mood of despair. They might believe they are helping you by pepping you up, saying something like, "Oh, c'mon, Joe. You have nothing to be unhappy about. Your wife is terrific. You've got a great job. Your children are good kids. I wish I had your life!"

If you've been putting on a good act, hiding your troubles behind a stiff upper lip, you might have to expect this. After all, how would the other person know that now you want to tell the truth? That your marriage is on the rocks, your job is unchallenging, your kids don't communicate with you. But once you do open the door to honesty and express what you feel, and why you feel that way, you might get some electrifying results.

Keep in mind, it will be not so much what *your friend* says, but what *you* discover about yourself in the process.

Which Friend to Go to as a Therapist

Having a human being who cares enough to listen to what is bothering you is essential to successful therapy.

So, before you go to a friend, remember it can't be just *any* friend. You want a friend who *listens*. Really listens. No interruptions, no tuning out, no cutting in on the tail end of your sentence. Those things indicate that your friend is not "there" for you.

Monica remembers a friend who was a "part-time" listener. "I would be telling her something, something especially meaningful to me, and all of a sudden she would interrupt with 'Do you want to go for ice cream later?' Or something equally inane. Yet, she was a friend. It's just that she wasn't a good listener. It was as if her concentration span just ran out of gas at a certain point. Then I realized it would be better to accept her as she was and take major problems to other friends."

You need a friend who will not become emotionally involved in the problem you are about to relate, sob, rant, or rave about. Some people have trouble understanding this important point. But if you have a friend who gallantly rushes to your side, takes your side and defends it—that won't help you at all. That kind of friend does not make a good therapist-friend.

Alex describes why. "I have a friend who no matter what problem I discuss will say, 'You mean that son of a bitch said [or did] that to you?' Forget it if I have a real problem with someone. Once I had a fight with the woman I was living with. I needed to talk to someone. I was upset. She wouldn't marry me because her career was important and she felt I would 'trap' her into some lifestyle with babies and all. I didn't want to do that. He told me she was one of those crazy women's libbers, not good enough for me, a bitch. About a week before that he was calling her the salt of the earth. I didn't want to hear those things, be cheered up. I wanted to understand her rejection so I could deal with it."

When someone like Alex's friend defends you by call-

ing someone else a son of a bitch or a crazy women's lib-
ber, you are talking to someone who is absolutely locked
into what I call value judgments. Though your friend may
passionately take your side, don't let loyalty fool you. Immediately discard the possibility of going to your personal
cheerleaders. They won't work for you as friend-therapists.

The reverse is true, as well. The friend who is quick to
criticize you and tell you where you have gone wrong is
not the friend you need in this instance. If you arrive with
your problem and are matter-of-factly greeted with "Listen, kid, life goes on. I knew it all along. I know we're
friends, but it was your fault," you did not pick the right
friend-therapist. Worse than a loyal cheerleader is a
friend who acts as judge and jury. Not only because it's so
disheartening, but because that type of person will know
the answer to your problem, to all problems, before you
even open your mouth. It's a snap decision and sentenc-
ing is very fast. He or she may mean well, but not do well.
Your friend's mind is made up as soon as you start bearing
your soul. It is doubtful if he or she is really listening to
you.

Professional therapists do nothing of the sort. They
have sometimes been called "sounding boards." For a
good reason. The friend who will function for you as therapist must have the ability to be almost a tape recorder.
Your friend must listen, record and play back so you can
hear it. Your friend must take an objective point of view.

Actually, one of the techniques a real therapist may indeed use is to repeat back to the patient, in a slightly different way, what has just been said. Often the patient is
so locked into a feeling about the statement that when he
or she hears the playback, there is an expression of surprise.

For instance, someone might say, "I must get out of this relationship."

The therapist answers, "You really must?"

The patient hears this and reflects, "Well, *must* is an awfully strong word. What I mean is . . ."

You begin to see how this process works. It takes the drama out of your statements and you begin to sift through to what is the reality of the situation. Now, you can't expect the same sort of insight you might get from a professional therapist to be readily available from a friend-therapist. But he or she *can* function in the same way.

Sandra says, "I have a good friend I go to with my problems. No matter what I choose to tell this person, first, she just listens. She happens to be very warm and understanding. Then she'll repeat some of it back to me. Like: 'Well, it sounds like you're very unhappy about such and such.' There is no emotionalism, no taking my side. Sometimes she will relate a similar experience to show what she's done. The point is when I come away, I know what to do about my problem. Or I see that it isn't that bad because I've gotten it off my chest."

Sandra's friend has the right idea and is a good friend-therapist. It is so easy to "preach" in a circumstance like this. Be very leery of a friend who is married to a rigid set of values. This is "right" and this is "wrong" and never, ever is there anything in between. Do not think of this person as a mature adult. Only children deal in black and whites—it's good or it's bad. Grown-ups realize, through life experiences, that there are subtle shadings. Perhaps only in instances of cold-blooded murder or other heinous crimes is there a universal sense of what is right and what is wrong.

For a friend to function as a therapist, he or she must

be beyond rigid absolutes and not puffed up with self-realized doctrines. This person might hold a PhD., or never have gone beyond high school. Education has nothing to do with it. Compassion, warmth, instinct, intuition, knowing just what to say at the right time are all human qualities. They are intangibles and can't be learned from books. Some people have these special qualities and others simply don't. You'll know who does. These people are easy to talk to.

Trust

You, must, of course, take into consideration the aspect of trust. Ethical therapists (and I like to think the vast majority are) respect what is called confidentiality. It means, simply, that the therapist never, never, never talks about his or her patients during a social evening, to a spouse, to another patient, to anyone at all.

If, to show an important point, a certain "case" is related, the specifics are so disguised—age, sex, etc.—as to render the person almost anonymous, and certainly unidentifiable by anyone who might also know the person in question.

However, a friend-therapist doesn't even have that luxury. Why not? Odds are the friend may move in the same social circles. Even if you find that special person who can listen and give objective feedback, do not minimize that important aspect of trust—unless you relish the thought of your private agonies being strewn about the social group in which you move.

I personally think that even more difficult than giving up cigarettes or sticking to a diet is keeping a personal confidence. John would agree. "There was a time in my life," he said, chuckling, "when I was holding so many people's secrets, I thought I would burst. Every other day one of my friends would call and say, 'Don't tell a soul, but . . .' Now, I consider myself a pretty conscientious person. Once, though, I got so confused I actually slipped and started to talk about one of those secrets because I forgot the other person didn't know. Fortunately, I found a way to cover it up."

John is unusual. He did it by accident. But you can imagine the temptation to gossip. Since the juicy little tidbits of life in any social group provide some of the more spicy and colorful moments, you will have to make sure your troubles aren't one of them. You might guard against this by prefacing your story with: "Don't tell anyone about this" or "I would appreciate this not going outside our conversation." Most likely your friend-therapist won't add you to the soap opera on the gossip circuit. But it pays to be cautious, for if your friend-therapist betrays your confidence, that friend is not only not a good friend-therapist, but not a good friend. It would be painful, while you are having problems, to add this discovery to them. A good clue to watch for is whether that friend provides you with enough material for a soap opera about *other people*.

Let's review the qualities a friend should have to be an effective friend-therapist:

1. The ability to be a good, sincere listener.
2. No emotional involvement in your problem.
3. An objective viewpoint.
4. The ability to keep your personal confidences.

The most capable practitioner of the art of being a friend-therapist will help you define the issues after listening to your high emotionalism without picking up on that emotionalism. The fact that this person is a friend

might be easier, and better, for you than facing a therapist. The therapist would be a stranger, probably
wouldn't be able to take you immediately, and would
have to get to know you before ever getting to your problem.

Asking

Now that you know the qualities you desire from a
friend-therapist and have found one, give yourself the
courage to go to that person.

It will take guts. You might think, "Oh, I can't go
through with this. What if I can't speak or I start to cry?"
You might fear the other person will think you are weak.
If it takes courage to dial a therapist and make an appointment, it takes just as much courage to dial a friend.

Silent arguments will prevent you from taking action.
You might tell yourself, "People should be able to handle
their own problems. I should be able to keep it all in."

My answer is, in a word—rubbish. No one can hold
everything in all the time, much less a major worry or
trouble. It is neither cool nor adult, but rather unhealthy,
time-consuming and energy-depleting. You are entitled
to have a problem and someone to talk to. This is not a
sign of weakness; it is a sign of humanness.

The best start, before you approach your friend, is to
name and describe your problem. That is the beginning
of any form of therapy. Before you go to your friend-therapist you have to be able to communicate your troubles.
If you have a general feeling of unhappiness or if many
things have gone wrong, this might be hard to do.

Ann-Marie sometimes falls into quicksand with her
emotions. A controlled young woman, she admits, "I have
a hard time getting angry at the moment something hap-

pens. I sort of gloss over it. So, it lingers inside me and I can't identify why I feel as I do later, except I feel off-kilter. That's what happens to my anger. My husband has learned this about me. If I can't find the words or get a start on explaining myself, he helps me by saying, 'Say anything that comes into your mind. Start by describing the way you feel.' Then what I'm really angry at will come out and we can unravel it."

If you are anything like Ann-Marie, if you feel your emotion strongly, but can't put it into words, try talking randomly into a tape recorder. Some people prefer to write out their feelings. One man confesses to keeping a notebook that he writes in whenever he's confused or unhappy. That's a form of therapy, too, but not the same as sharing a problem with another person. So, if your problem is a little confusing even to you, make sure you can relate it. Don't rehearse it, just define it.

Keep in mind, too, that while a therapist is paid to listen to your problems, a friend isn't. You make an appointment to see a therapist. You may have to ask for your friend's time in the same way . . . especially with a busy friend. Make an appointment if you have to.

Louise, who was having terrible troubles planning a wedding her parents didn't really approve of, called her friends and simply said, "Do you have a few minutes for a friend?" Then she launched into her agonies, trying to find a solution to what should be the happiest day of her life. A few listened, really listened, and she was able to come away feeling she should and could plan her own wedding.

You might also call the friend and begin by saying, "Hey, can you act as a therapist for me? I've got this awful problem and I'd appreciate it if you would hear me out." You can talk over the phone, which is more comfortable and immediate for some, or make an appointment to meet. This is a far better way to begin than dropping a bombshell on someone by opening with, for example: "Hello, Sue. This is Jane. I'm leaving Henry . . ."

You might warn the person you're liable to cry, chain-smoke, get drunk, rip little pieces of paper. After you have told your problem, don't apologize for it. If you feel guilty, remember the old cliché, "What are friends for?" You show your appreciation for your friend's time and ear by offering yours sometime.

Keep in mind everything your friend has said during and after your telling. Be careful of any advice, no matter how sound. It took me years to realize that there is no real advice one can give to another. The individual truth for every single one of us lies deep inside. A friend-therapist can get to that inner truth in you only by asking questions and simply listening.

So, if the friend-therapist you selected does nothing more than dole out advice, your plan backfired. After all, if you wanted that, you could have written Ann Landers. There's no law that says you can't find another friend-therapist if you've spilled your guts to one and are dissatisfied. Why not go on to another friend?

To try to help you further, here are more specific guidelines on how to determine whether your friend will function as a capable friend-therapist. Answer all of the following questions with either yes or no. Keep only one friend in mind at a time, then match the answers you get with the answers at the end of the quiz.

Can a Friend Be a Therapist?

1. Do you generally feel *comfortable* in your friend's company?
2. Does your friend ever tell you confidences of other friends? Is your friend a great gossip?

3. Will he or she chance to gain or lose by your problem?
4. Does he or she really listen?
5. Is your friend judgmental about others, seeming to have all the answers to life's problems?
6. Does you friend possess good old-fashioned "horse sense"?
7. Does he or she genuinely like you?
8. Has your friend ever surprised you with sudden acts of hostility?
9. Is your friend "shock-proof?" In other words, can you tell him or her unusual information and will it be taken in stride?
10. Does your friend get a personal kick out of life?

Correct answers to the above questions are 1) Yes 2) No 3) No 4) Yes 5) No 6) Yes 7) Yes 8) No 9) Yes 10) Yes.

Number 10, to be sure, is a loaded question. It is important that you answer it for each friend you are testing. For if the person you want to entrust with your troubles is in a sad state of being heavily influenced by his or her own emotions, or is generally negative, this person is not a wise choice.

A question, I imagine, may have popped into your mind during this chapter. Are you wondering why someone who is a practicing psychotherapist would recommend that you *not* see one if it can be prevented?

I have sometimes seen people for just a few visits who did not need treatment, but who came to me because they had "no one to talk to." I felt it was a waste to subject this type of person to the rigidity of office sessions and hours. Also, such is the way of our modern civilization that when we need professional guidance, we must make an appointment in advance. It may not be a time when we feel especially comfortable talking; it may be inconvenient to our schedules and we may have to take time off from work. People who have more serious or clinical problems must adjust to these facts of life. But people who have life problems that have no underlying causes that require treatment are merely purchasing the services of a friend.

I do see, however, in my practice, many people who have friends who are judgmental, freely dispense advice, and are unable to be objective. These people are friends who like to run others' lives. My patients come to me to break these imagined, but very real ropes, so they can learn to grow and grow up. Do you have people in your life who are running it?

Chapter VI
How to Stop Friends from Running Your Life

"A day for toil, an hour for sport, but for a friend is life too short."

—Emerson, "Considerations
   by the Way"

It's a contradiction, isn't it? First we agree friends are prized. People who offer a closeness that is to be treasured and who define our sense of self-esteem. Now, we introduce another point of view that must be considered. Some friends, though they provide comfort, actually rob us of our self-esteem, and the closeness is illusory. What kinds of friends are these? How does this happen?

Without knowing it, we seem to pass through life carefully duplicating what went on in our childhood. Not because it worked so well, but because that is what we are used to. Often, that is how we choose our friends. Almost everyone has a friend who possesses the same qualities either Mommy or Daddy had. This is especially true if our parents live far away or have died. Love relationships often pick up this continuing thread, and friendships are no different.

Odds are if you had a strong, domineering parent who

115

told you what to wear, what college to attend, what food to eat, you are doing one of two things: You have a friend or friends you delight in "taking charge of " and are, quite naturally, a *controller*. Or, the reverse. You assume the role of the child in a friendship and are the *controlled*. You cannot make a decision unless you consult your controlling friend of the moment. On a minor level, you may be content to let your friend choose the movie, the restaurant, the activity, and go along good-naturedly. It's less trouble for you that way, you think.

If you didn't have a domineering parent, most likely you won't want a friend who will act as a parent to you. But often, if you had a weak parent, you will set up the need to find a parent out in the world and you may very well gravitate to a "voice of authority" in your life. So, it works many ways.

All children, early on, make life decisions concerning their relationships with parents, depending on what it is safe to do. If a parent is a bully, a child learns to shut up and play it cool. If a parent is open and loving, the child responds the same way. This sets the tone for our grown-up friendships, a pattern we continue but can break if we understand it and want to.

This chapter is dedicated to those who can admit they are controlled, to any degree, by friends or a friend and would like to change. If this is not you, before you flip on, remember that when I say controlled, I am including subtle nuances. Examples may be extreme to clarify a definition, but you may find yourself somewhere here. Or, you may detect that you are something of a *controller*, though no one has spelled it out quite that way for you. You might want to know how your friends feel, truthfully, about this aspect of your personality. Or, how you may be preventing the adult in them to emerge and take responsibility. You may also wish to know that such words as *controller* and *controlled* do not, in fact, belong in the same vocabulary as friendship. They are merely games people construct out of habit. If you assume the role of *controller* or *controlled*, you are not really enjoying friendship in the best sense of the word. You are not really a friend.

There is often a slender, almost invisible line that marks the boundary between a healthy and unhealthy friendship. Time and time again, I meet people whose relationships with friends are frustrating, disappointing or deeply unsatisfactory. Often the person can't tell the difference between a healthy and an unhealthy friendship.

Actually, it's not that difficult to diagnose. In a healthy friendship, one enjoys just "being there," part of a balanced give-and-take. In an unhealthy friendship, the relationship is unbalanced, perhaps with one person dependent on the other's *approval*. Oddly enough, it's entirely possible to care deeply for a close friend but be unhappy in the relationship.

Not long ago Deborah sat in my living room clenching her fists in frustration. "I'll never learn," she moaned. "I went and did it again!"

What Deborah had done, and fortunately was well aware of, was to once again allow her friend, Carrie, to talk her into something. This time, it was expensive and temporarily irreversible—spanking new red and white striped wallpaper for her kitchen. "We went together to pick it out. Carrie loved it, said it would perk up the whole room. I went along. Now it's *me* who has to fry eggs in that candy-striped prison. I hate it! I'll never get used to it."

At least, though, Deborah didn't blame Carrie. That's something different. No, she put the blame squarely on a problem of hers—coming under the thumb of the domineering Carrie. Deborah lets herself be controlled and is beginning to realize it. Obviously she finds her deep woman-to-woman friendship with Carrie rich and rewarding. In some ways. In her zeal to do everything possible to preserve this special relationship, she lets herself fall prey to the more controlling personality of Carrie, who is also desperately trying to fulfill her own needs.

Deborah realized she wasn't just angry about the choice of wallpaper. She was furious with herself for again letting Carrie's judgment override her own. Carrie had felt her kitchen was dark and dismal; the snappy wallpaper would brighten it up. It was Carrie, also, who had said Deborah's child was overweight, urging her to put him on a diet, and that her house was too small, which resulted in a costly addition. At first, Deborah saw Carrie as an expert on every subject, much the same way a child views a parent.

When Deborah came to see me she realized she had problems simply because she was unhappy. She suspected some of her troubles stemmed from her friendships. Gradually, she pinpointed most of it to what Carrie represented in her life. "Should I drop her as a friend?" she asked me. It was evident that a cold-turkey sacrifice wouldn't solve her problem. I suggested there was an alternative. What would happen if Deborah stopped acting blindly on Carrie's advice? Instead, what if she stopped and thought it over—didn't do what Carrie said if she didn't want to? Deborah was dumbfounded. The rules of the relationship, though unspoken, were now clear to her. How could she break out of the role she had been playing and still remain a friend to the overpowering Carrie?

Deborah's biggest problem was to learn to respect her own opinions, previously censored by Carrie, and by a chain of similar people in her past. She made real progress when she bought a pair of high-heeled shoes Carrie had labeled "too high and too expensive." "I almost let her talk me out of them," Deborah recalled. "But I bought them because I wanted them, and you should have seen Carrie's face!" The funniest thing of all to Deborah was that eventually Carrie ended up with the same pair, because they were the fashion.

Not all of us have controlling friendships that have gone this far, to be sure. We may allow ourselves, at certain times in our lives, to be controlled by some friends and not others. Though this is certainly not exclusively a woman's problem, brought on by old-fashioned conditioning that signals them to be compliant, I do think fewer men are apt to be controlled by friends. At least in the same definable way. Mostly, I believe this is because men just don't get as intimate with their friends. Men have yet to master the totally honest give-and-take that could allow this problem to arise.

What Deborah has begun to do is change the boundaries in a relationship with a woman she still considers a good friend. To end her friendship and run away would not solve her problem. There would be other Carries and she would have to deal with them. Deborah will have to pass through several developing stages before she is able to break Carrie's controlling influence completely, and relate as an equal and True-Blue Friend.

There are several ways the controller is *used* in this type of relationship, as well.

Using a Friend as a Parent

Susan is a young woman who *allows* a friend to run her life. Unlike Deborah, who did not invite it, Susan literally asks for control. When her garbage-disposal unit broke down, Susan called her best friend, Marsha, to ask her what to do. When a magazine subscription expired, she consulted Marsha before she renewed it. When undecided as to what to make for dinner, she would phone Marsha to see what she was having. Marsha had always played her motherly role to perfection until one day when everything went wrong. One of her children had slipped and gashed an arm so that stitches had to be taken, the baby had been screaming all day, and when Susan called, there was a cooking fire on the stove. Marsha found herself, nerves frazzled, muttering sternly, "Oh, for heaven's sake, Susan, can't you think for yourself? Just this once!" And she hung up.

Marsha had slipped out of the role Susan expected her to play. Susan was deeply hurt by this unexpected rebuttal. "I thought Marsha was my friend," she said in disbelief.

Susan is a striking example of an adult woman who needs a mommy. Some of us have this need to a lesser degree. In Susan's case, her friend was willing to play Mommy until the day came when Marsha needed a Mommy herself!

Donna, a young woman in her late twenties, was getting dressed to go to a singles dance when the phone rang. It was a girlfriend who was going to the same party but wanted to know if she should wear her pink outfit. This was a woman who was beginning to call Donna two and three times a day about similar matters of unimportance. One morning while Donna was scrambling eggs the phone in the kitchen rang. Sure enough, it was her friend calling to ask what she should take for diarrhea. Donna threw her eggs in the wastebasket. She wanted to stop the pattern so when this woman called to ask which outfit would be best for a dinner party, Donna said, matter-of-factly, "I'm sorry. I just can't answer that for you." That one sentence made it quite clear she would not take over the role of parent. She didn't need it. Unfortunately, many people do.

Ray decided to buy a used car. He took his friend Stanley along, who considered himself something of a car expert, as insurance against "getting taken." Stanley advised him to get a Pinto; there was nothing else worthwhile on the lot. Ray really wanted an AMC Pacer. Both cars were in good condition. Before Ray knew it, they were arguing about it. Suddenly he had an insight—was one car really better than the other, or, in bringing Stanley along as an expert, had he set up a situation in which Stanley had to control?

Friends are not parents. It is not their duty to guide and protect us. They can be supportive but they cannot offer unlimited help *and* be a friend. One way of checking yourself to see if you are casting any of your friends in the role of parent is to keep track of how many times you phone that person and how many phone calls are to get an answer or advice about something that is, really, trivial.

If you seek your friend's advice on even the smallest matters, your behavior is more like that of a toddler than a peer. You will be a step closer to growing up, as Deborah did, if you merely realize what you are doing.

Using a Friend as a Catalyst

Occasionally people use a friend's advice as a catalyst to action—and then proceed to blame the results on the guiltless person who gave them the advice. This can go to ridiculous extremes.

A prime example is a man who had written a novel. Edgar had several friends whom he asked to read it and give him suggestions. Before he took these people's suggestions, he would weigh their importance or intelligence. One friend in the publishing business told him quite honestly that he should get a literary agent. That was the best way to sell his book. Edgar responded to his friend's advice and eagerly accepted a carefully drawn up list of agents. For months, he took the manuscript around to agent after agent, instead of to publishers, waited for the agents to find the time to read it, and was rejected time and again. He finally decided that these agents didn't want to bother with beginning novelists. He blamed his friend for sending him on a time-consuming wild goose chase. His friend should have known. But he never blamed himself, never considered for a moment that perhaps his novel was not good enough.

A middle-aged woman, Helen, agonized over whether to separate from her husband. Although he had been unfaithful several times, he was a good provider and a loving father. She went from friend to friend asking each one, "What should I do?" Most of them said quite frankly that they didn't feel they could give advice, didn't know what to say, but they did offer warmth and sympathy. Finally Helen found what she was looking for. One friend, Johanna, said, "I can't imagine how you could stay married to a man who is having affairs right under your nose!" This was the green light Helen had been waiting for. She left her husband.

Months later, she had a change of heart. She felt leaving her husband had been a terrible mistake; she would never have done it but for Johanna. She comforted herself with the delusion that it was Johanna's bad decision, not hers, that led to the breakup of her marriage. You can't blame another for anything, really. It suited Helen to blame her friend, yet ultimately our behavior is our own. No one makes you do anything!

Common sense dictates that if you are willing to abdicate to another person's advice, then you should take responsibility for the action, not blame the person for the bad decision. Yet, how many people, consciously or unconsciously, do this? In reality, friends cannot run, or ruin, your life unless you let them. We give them the power to act.

When people cannot make their own decisions, it is because this thinking process is like an unused muscle. Some people were so bossed from the time they were little that they never learned to think, feel, or intuit for themselves. Unfortunately, the parent stepped in and said too often, too loudly, "I know better." One doesn't arrive at eighteen or twenty-one or thirty-five and suddenly know how to make decisions for oneself. It takes practice, learning and sometimes falling down.

We are so afraid of making mistakes. What is a mistake? Nothing. I have no definition. You do what you do at any stage or moment of your life because that is all you can do. We learn; we go on to another, wiser level. Don't look back and call a behavior a "mistake." That's the only mistake.

Using a Friend as a Master

What about the irresistible, charismatic, dominating friend who wants to run your life and takes over, even in small ways, very efficiently? Sometimes there's not too much opposition because the person is so overpowering and it's just too much trouble to confront him or her at every turn.

The master isn't necessarily a bully. The master can be subtle, yet powerful. When you go out for Chinese food, for example, the master will order for everyone before you know what happened.

Carolyn, a young mother of three, was under the influence of a woman of this type. New to the neighborhood, Carolyn was eager to make friends. Into her life came Lilah who, like a mother hen, took Carolyn under her wing. Soon Carolyn discovered that there were queen bee as well as mother hen facets to Lilah's personality. Lilah was the community's social arbiter; her friends and their husbands were the "in" group, all the others were "out."

"I just loved Lilah at first," Carolyn told me. "I was her special pal. But before I knew it, I was doing whatever she wanted me to do. Sometimes I feel as if I am being squashed by her, but I don't know what to do. I want to keep her as my friend, because I really like her, but I'm beginning to not like myself for just going along."

A master/slave relationship may have its rewards. Perhaps the weaker person enjoys being dominated—to a point. But let's not make the mistake of calling this friendship. Carolyn found out that if she truly wanted a friendship with Lilah or anyone else, she would have to teach herself to give as well as take, to lead as well as follow. It meant figuring out what she really wanted to do and acting on it.

Sometimes in adulthood we feel as weak and frightened as we may have in childhood. We may so want to reach out and be truly accepted by another human being, escape loneliness, feel that someone is ours, that we entrap ourselves in the master/slave friendship. We think this will bring us close to someone, the way a mother is to a baby. But it won't. It may seem to, for a time, but then the fact that you are not a baby but twenty-five or thirty-five or forty-five gets in the way and you rebel. Slaves have a way of rebelling against their masters.

The only way out of your dilemma is to become your own person. What a deliciously easy phrase to write, and oh, how difficult to live. I wrestle with it, often. The fact is you are many persons. Your center is like the center of a wheel. All the spokes are the myriad parts of you. Watch, observe, love all your many facets instead of judging some as good and some as bad. If you have one spoke that needs to be continually fixed, so be it—until the day when you don't have to do that anymore. Try to be aware of who you are and what you want.

If you're unhappy because you think a friend is running your life, your first task is to start *thinking for yourself*. It's simple unless you've lost touch with your feelings and your intuition. So many people have lost the ability to go with a true emotion, or even recognize it. They think they're content having someone else run the whole show and then they wake up one morning and don't know why they're angry. That's the time to take your first steps. After-the-fact resentment is commonplace when you are letting yourself be controlled.

We have two sides to our brain: the left side, which focuses on analytical reasoning and thinking, and the right side, which is intuitive and creative. Because we have received such powerful admonitions to think, many of us have a hard time acting on intuition, which is sometimes the wiser course. Only *you* can tell if you have been playing the role of the *controlled*. But it is in your power to begin again. Use your intuition and your creativity and start changing your future and yourself.

Breaking the Pattern

Here is an exercise to practice on paper before you apply it to your friendships. Fill it in for only one friend at a time. Then do it over again for another friend or friends.

Answer the following questions. Do it for one friend or several.

1. Why have I chosen _____ for a friend? What rewards do I get from the friendship? What pain do I get? Are they equal?

2. Pick out your current problem, think about it for just a moment, now fill in the name of your closest friend _____ and imagine what that person might say in response to the problem. (Often we don't realize how well we know the other person's thinking.)

This exercise has a second part; imagine *your* response to the problem. Does it mesh with what you think your friend's response would be?

3. The next time you are upset and tempted to run immediately to the telephone to call a friend for advice, turn away from the telephone and sit down in the most comfortable chair in the house. Put your hands on your knees, uncross your legs and relax your body. Sit with your feet firmly planted on the floor. Now close your eyes and see yourself in your favorite place of relaxation. This may be a beach you've been on, a treehouse in childhood, or a faraway imaginary oasis. Repeat to yourself, after you feel relaxed, "I have time to make this decision." (If you are with too many people or too much noise, lock yourself in the bathroom.)

4. Make a list of the close friends who influence your life now. Jot down next to each name how you feel after you talk to that particular friend . . . happy, quiet, depressed, angry, let down, lifted up.

5. Using the same list of friends, describe in two words what each friend adds to your life. Or doesn't. Put in the negatives as well.

6. If a friendship you like has bogged down with "heavy" advice or control, plan a lunch or excursion together that is creative enjoyment for both of you. Resolve to enjoy yourself with your old friend in a new way; don't just sit there and hash over problems or be lured by advice. Expand the relationship to include new topics; I call this "looking out" together instead of focusing in.

7. List the major decisions in which you have let a friend run your life. Now, did it work?

8. This exercise I call doing research. With a specific problem, call every single friend you know and ask your friend how to solve it. Jot down on a piece of paper just a couple of key words so you'll remember what each person said. (What you will begin to see in your role as a researcher is that the friends you call all have *their* opinion, based upon *their* beliefs, feelings and attitudes. And that may or may not have anything at all to do with you.)

9. Tune up your listening powers by watching for phrases like *you should, you shouldn't, you ought to, you must.* What you are doing is honing in on what I term "parent words," the kind mothers and fathers use with their children, and when you listen, it will become very clear to you how some friends love to play that parent role in your life. (And obviously a part of you enjoys playing the child role, or you wouldn't be putting up with it!)

10. Tell the friend who has been most dominant in running your life how much you appreciate him/ her being in your life, that you feel that you share something valuable, but that you are in the process of thinking and making more decisions for yourself. Say it in a friendly way, say it truthfully and say it with determination. Most interesting will be the response you'll get. Jot it down.

11. Is there a friend with whom none of this will work, whom you may have to cross out of your life? If so, see the next chapter.

12. The most important point is last: Ask yourself if you love yourself. This is the Big Truth. You are an okay person and you must agree. But if this Big Truth gets hidden behind the debris of self-criticism, self-loathing, self-destructiveness, you cannot allow yourself to bask in the self-love we have discussed. Self-love is the first requirement for *wholeness*. Without it you will be unduly tossed or swayed and will deliver yourself to another human being. Work on the Self-Love Exercises in Chapter II every day.

One clue to friendships that involve controlling roles was mentioned in this chapter. Did you catch it?

It was simply this: Friends who control are not True-Blue Friends. Once you liberate yourself from the games you once thought necessary, a magical thing happens. The give-and-take becomes more equal.

"But where do I begin?" you might ask. You begin with awareness of what is happening, observation as it happens, and a desire not to be controlled. Then utilize the exercises in this chapter. As you practice gaining confidence in yourself, it will become easier and you will be your own person in your friendships.

Keep those same friends in your life, if you can, but assert yourself. See yourself as an adult. Abbie tells the story of a very shaky time in her life. "I was depressed. There was nothing more I could do, I figured, than just ride it and try to act normal. During this time, I tried to go out socially as much as possible. It helped me to be with people. I had a new friend at the time who made this very convenient. She always wanted to go out. Though I soon realized she was picking all the places, I went along.

"But as the depression began to lift, I began to rebel. It was easier for me at the time to drop her. I could have asserted myself or confronted her. I'm at the top of her enemy list, I guess. Since she's not especially my type of person, perhaps the friendship would have dissolved anyway, but at the time I despised her for not being able to see what was happening. Now, from what I hear, she still doesn't really understand. Knowing what I know now, I might have handled it much differently."

Should you avoid all strong personality types when you choose new friends? Absolutely not. You can learn to temper their influence, and what better way than to *practice* on the controlling friends you have now. A dominating person can be an exciting friend. Especially if you stand up for yourself.

Welcome the opportunity to gain new friends and handle your old friends as you become your own person. Take it as a challenge. Do it with a sense of humor, if that's your style. Why not? You could call up a friend, whom you've let control you, and say, "I have a disaster. I have no decisions for you to make for me today. What do you think of that?"

Indeed, what will your friend think of that?

And why don't *you* think of this poem every so often:

Don't walk in front of me
I may not follow
Don't walk behind me
I may not lead
Walk beside me
And just be my friend.

—Albert Camus

If your controlling friend can't accept that, you will have to end the friendship. Because if you want to be equal in friendship and your friend wants you to "walk behind," there is no friendship.

Chapter VII
When a Friendship is not Forever—and What to Do

"God gives us relatives; thank God, we can choose our friends."

—Addison Miszner,
The Cynics' Calendar

Some people would use the word *terminate*, but I hesitate to do that. Not only because of its harshness and finality, but because I picture *terminated* stamped in big block letters on a file. And because we are dealing with what was once, at least, a very special human relationship, a friendship.

To talk about ending a friendship, even gracefully, may seem like heresy to many. For isn't friendship synonymous with loyalty? We think, "How difficult he or she has become, but . . . that was the person who pulled me through my depression six years ago and I'll never forget it." Or, "Our mothers were best friends. We grew up together. We must be friends." *How can I cut a person like this out of my life? I can't.*

The answer to this is simply that if you feel so strongly about it, you can't. At least not at this very moment. But you know in your mind and heart, as you learn more about

131

friendship, that beginnings and endings are part and parcel of the process. There may come a day when you cannot, and will not, be saddled with tired relationships and you will want an easy, honest, graceful way to move on. We do this in love affairs—why should friendships be different?

Your feelings of loyalty may not be so strong at a certain time that you are completely willing to spend time with a person who hasn't grown the way you have, whose life is traveling in a different direction. If you are honest with yourself, that time might be now with one or more of your friends.

It happens to more and more people every day, whether they recognize it or not. When everyone grew up, married, and died in the same, comfortable neighborhoods (the good old days), people rarely examined relationships the way we do today. A book like this would have been impossible. Because then you had ready-made friends. They went through school with you, came to your wedding, and your families all knew each other. Maybe your children played together. Very few friends were chosen or courted; they just seemed to be there. No wonder we have inherited the tendency to take friendship for granted.

Today it's different. More people move to other neighborhoods or cities as their careers change. More people move to find a spot where the social life swings. People have moved from suburb to city and back again. People move to warmer climates, retire to other locations. With all this mobility comes change. And growth. People who remained in the same neighborhoods merely grew up in terms of age, but now we *grow*, and the word has an all-new meaning in our vocabulary. In the context in which I mean it to be interpreted, it has been much misunderstood and misused.

My definition of growth is: Not clinging to the ideas, beliefs, or ways of being in the world that we grew up with or were taught. *Unless they work now.* Knowing that leaving that old, safe space of do's and don'ts, rights and wrongs, involves some risk, but being willing to do it anyway for the reward of growth. Seeing every day as new and fresh. Delighting in anything and everything. With growth, you enjoy more self-love and love of others.

You do not need physical movement to grow. It is possible, with the right attitude, to stay in the same city, keep the same job, have the same group of friends and grow. Growth takes place inwardly. After that it expresses itself outwardly, so that others may notice. We see this plainly in children as they pass from tots to teens to young adults. Adults can do it, too.

You might have grown without even knowing it. While you are exploring and experiencing new risks and challenges, someone you've considered a friend hasn't, and gets left behind. That person's conversation may not interest you as much as it once did. His or her company may even bore you. The camaraderie, the honesty, have vanished. Where was that wavelength you both were on?

People ask themselves the question, "Did *they* change or did *I*?" The correct answer is—you both did. In a sense. You grew and your friend didn't. Your friend stayed the same or, in your eyes, may even have slipped backward. Most likely, you've both grown—but in *different* directions. Perhaps you're immersed in an active single life and your friend is married and occupied with raising a family. Obviously, you've both changed. Your values are different.

You may feel remorse or guilt for your feelings. *My God, that person used to be my best friend. My very best friend.*

How can this be happening?

It is. Friendships are born and die just as human beings come into the world and leave it.

Gertrude Stein created one of her marvelously original titles on this subject: "Before the Flowers of Friendship Faded Friendship Faded." She had translated a poem for a friend who felt she had taken liberties with it and they parted in anger.

But not all friendships end as dramatically as that. Mostly we are talking of a reverse of the poet's title: "Before the Friendship Faded, the Flowers of Friendship Faded." Nothing has been said, but the friendship's wilted, has lost its bloom, died. You may be the only one aware that it has become a skeleton of what it once was.

I had that exact problem this year. An old friend of mine came to visit. We go back a long time and share many good experiences. She had long ago divorced her husband and is now living with someone who will never make my gallery of favorite persons. He is a hostile, angry, sullen man-child. Three thousand miles across the country, she called me long-distance to reserve my company for dinner when she arrived in the city.

We met and greeted one another at a quaint little French restaurant I had carefully selected; I was looking forward to a nice meal even though her lover was accompanying us. Not long after the water glasses were placed on the table, she began to argue with him. He shouted back. I found myself playing the role of arbitrator, which was certainly not conducive to the charming, friendly meal I had been looking forward to. It seemed to me three voices, and only three, filled the room as other guests looked away discreetly.

Afterward, I figured I had no one to blame but myself. I knew what her boyfriend was like. I could have said, "No, let's make it another time, when you're alone." The dinner would have been different if it had been just us. I treasured the friendship I thought still lived. This was shattered by a phone call from her. She apologized and admitted that the only reason they had met me for dinner was so I could act as the dupe because she wanted to argue with him in the company of another woman. I couldn't believe it. First, I was furious with her. Second, I was angry at myself for being so blind and letting myself fall into a trap.

I tried to calm my anger by reminding myself to forgive and forget. This was a friend I had had for over twenty years. *Over twenty years* kept crisscrossing my mind.

Until it dissolved. I realized even the words didn't work. The truth was the friendship, lovely and close as it had once been, simply had not survived the years. In my heart I felt it was dead. If I had any further doubts, they were silenced once and for all by yet another call from her. She wanted to rehash everything that had gone on. We had really grown apart, I felt, but all I said was, "No, I have nothing to talk about. Consider the incident over. Please." Then I added softly, as if in reassurance, "You are my friend. You always will be."

Later on, after I hung up, I realized how guilt-ridden was that reflexive "You are my friend, you always will be." It wasn't true. She was no longer my friend. We had not really shared interests or lifestyles for many years. It was only in my mind that I thought of her as a friend. In reality, she was the least likely person I would want to be friends with as I am now.

Like many other people, I like an act of closing, a finality, like the last chapter of a book. I sat down and wrote her an angry letter telling her how much I disliked what she had done. That I didn't consider us friends anymore. Then, fortunately, I ripped it up. It was enough for me to know in my heart that the friendship was over, to know that the next time she wanted to meet me for dinner my answer would be, "I'm sorry, but I can't make it. I'm busy."

I do wish her well. She is now a Former Friend. That she has neither the insight nor the intuition to see this, that I feel she does not really value my friendship, is all the more reason to reclassify her.

Still, some may argue that long-term friends are to be carried forever, as one carries an indigent aunt and uncle and pays their rent. No one can sway them. But when you assess the relationships in your life, you may find too much of your time is spent propping up dying relationships that rob you of time you could spend with new, stimulating friends.

This Is the Time to End a Friendship

It was a stormy summer Sunday and Elizabeth was working on an oil painting, her first. She felt relaxed in her solitude, her aloneness. In the background, the stereo played some of her favorite music. In the refrigerator was a fresh pitcher of iced tea. She was enjoying herself.

Interrupting this peaceful reverie was the demanding chime of her doorbell. Probably a neighbor who needed to borrow something. She went to answer it and her mouth dropped open. It was a friend she hadn't seen in months who lived nearby. Her eyes opened wide and all she could do was stare.

"Hyee!" Her friend smiled. "It's pouring and I decided to stop in and dry off. The downstairs door was open." Elizabeth noticed she was wearing a very sturdy, hooded plastic raincoat. She wasn't even wet. "Well, can't I come in?"

Elizabeth felt trapped. As if someone had cut off her

fun and she was stuck. "Okay, but I'm working on something so I can't spend all day chatting." That, thought Elizabeth, should do it.

It didn't. Two hours later, when the pitcher of iced tea was drained, after many more-than-gentle hints, her friend finally decided that she had killed enough time between activities and she would go home and do the laundry.

Elizabeth remembers feeling a wonderful lift when she was alone again, but also feeling she had been cheated of two precious hours. Then she realized that she was not really friends with this woman anymore. Elizabeth said, "It's so obvious she popped over because, though she's not open and honest, she was making some kind of an attempt to revive our friendship. But her attempt was terrible. I hate it when people ring my doorbell and take me by surprise. So, I sat there and listened to her chat and I thought, 'I don't like her. I just don't like this type of person.' And I don't feel guilty about it anymore. Just being with her that one day made me feel depressed and angry."

Knowing precisely when a friendship is over is a "gut" feeling. Your own. All you have to do is recognize that feeling. In a controller-controlling relationship, as mentioned in Chapter VI, it might not be possible to redefine and save the relationship. If you work with it and it doesn't work, you'll know when to give up.

You may also have had, at some time in your life, a person who was a "mentor," someone who helped you and freely guided you along. But one day, like a person who does not want to be controlled, you grow up, are able to fly on your own wings, yet the friendship cannot. You must end the mentor/student friendship if it doesn't grow with you or if you outgrow it.

There is another friendship best left behind because it is destructive to you. Dr. Herbert Otto labels it the Energy-Vampire Relationship. He described this friendship as one in which one person is able to draw energy from the other, but the person being used is left drained, depressed, devitalized. Apparently, this forms the basis for many friendships until people learn to recognize what is happening.

A woman in her mid-forties told Dr. Otto in an agitated tone of voice, "I can't believe what you just said about the Energy-Vampire thing. For the last twenty years I have had a friendship with a woman who visits me maybe every five or six months. She lives in a small town and is bored. I know I've helped her a lot over the years and she seems to listen to me when I talk, but she always comes up with new problems and difficulties every time she visits. This has been going on for as long as we've been friends and I always feel drained when she leaves. The last two or three visits I've actually had to go to bed for a couple of days. Now I realize what's been happening. I wasn't coming down with a cold or a virus. I was pouring my energy down the drain!"

This would be a good time for this woman to end the friendship. Unfortunately, life situations aren't always this easy to figure out. There are times when you know you want to end a friendship, but there are overlapping threads that leave you confused. Perhaps a further discussion of various other ways friendships end might help to unravel any loose ends.

The Success Syndrome

Tom Powers, a Pulitzer Prize-winning journalist, wrote in *Ms.* magazine (January 1975) about the tension between men who have made it and men who feel they have not. Certainly, this same Success Syndrome that often makes male friendship awkward can be translated to women as well. Powers came to this conclusion: "I do not think we mind so much what others do as what *we* have not done, that we are less envious of success than diminished by our own failure."

Powers maintains that the successful person (interpret success in any way you choose) will find that old friends call less frequently, expect the person to talk about what he or she is doing, and then are vague or embarrassed about what they themselves are up to. Society is cruel in dividing us into winners and losers. John Wayne once said to Richard Nixon at a fund-raising benefit, "You were a winner and then a loser and now you're a winner again." Powers claims it is not the winners in life who forget their old friends so much as the losers who feel they must withdraw. This is not so much from envy or bitterness as from their sense of awkward inadequacy. Would it be painful if your friend became a Justice on the Supreme Court while you went no further than your own law practice? Would it be hard to take if an old friend from little theater became a movie star but you never made it? Would you avoid a friend who became fabulously wealthy if you knew you would have to be content with a middle-class income for the rest of your life?

According to Powers, it is impossible for men to talk this over and bring it out into the open. "How would you tell an old friend," he says, "that you understand why he is tongue-tied with you, that failure has sometimes infected your spirit, but you like him anyway, don't give a damn whether he's done the vast things he wanted to do, that you sympathize with his disappointment and understand the shrinkage of his ambition?" It would be an insult to the man's dignity, Powers feels.

While I sympathize with Power's careful respect for a man's dignity, I can only regret this type of reasoning.

Winners and losers, like controllers and controlling, have no place in the friendship vocabulary. Winning could be refinishing a chair beautifully. Losing is up to the person who lost to define, and to deal with. True friendship requires true openness.

This friend would continually call Gold in the middle of the night, long-distance, waking up his wife to talk out his visions. He said over the telephone once:

> "I'd like to come and stay with you awhile till I get my head together. You're my only friend. The rest are working for . . . you know, Herb."
>
> "Uh," I said, which is already the beginning of the way you don't talk to a friend—thinking of ways to escape. "Uh, we're kind of busy right now."

Gold's friend then pleads with him that all the resorts are controlled by Washington. That he has been told to go to a hospital, but thinks he just needs a rest. To all of which Gold can only reply, "Uh."

Gold reflects on this man, with whom he had shared so many nice experiences and who he now knew was in bad trouble.

Finally he resolves his conflict: "I'm sorry, Hank," he said.

Hank was striking that familiar chord with Gold—it's time to end the friendship. Not because Gold was a Fairweather Friend. He had, after all, been at the other end of the line in the wee hours of the morning for him and truly cared about his friend's illness. Gold felt that this man was an intelligent adult who had gotten himself into his own kind of trouble by behaving unintelligently. Gold couldn't go any further without hurting himself.

To drop a friend in failure can be cruel or honest and self-protective. If friends demand too much of you, as Gold's friend did, sometimes you must be kind to yourself and cruel to them. It is far worse to succumb to the burdening request out of a feeling of duty, and end up not being able to cope with the situation.

If you drop a friend as soon as you get the news that he or she has been in a car accident and won't make this season's skiing with you—that is cruel. Ending a friendship with someone who has pushed his or her self-destructive button, or whom you have outgrown, is your prerogative. How do you know the difference? You'll know in your heart at the time.

Triangles

A friendship can end, too, in the sense that it will never be the same, when best friends or roommates are forced to separate because one finds a lover or gets married. The person left behind can feel like a fifth wheel. This is called the Triangle—love splits a friendship. The friendship doesn't have to die, but it usually begins to fade, no longer flourishing in the same way it did before the third person entered the picture.

Two young women who both had interesting jobs shared a nice apartment, their vacations, their ups and downs, their wardrobes, and were "like sisters," they were fond of saying, until one of them, Shelly, met a man. Not just any man, but the man she wanted to marry. He was not only a lover, but a friend as well. Immediately, Jean felt left out. Then she felt threatened when she realized Shelly was really serious about this man. All too soon, it seemed, they broke up the apartment, Jean was maid-of-honor at Shelly's wedding, and was waving goodbye when they left for their honeymoon. She felt lost and lonely. No casual friend or date could fill the void that was left in her life.

Shelly remembers the day she got married. "It should have been the happiest day of my life, but it was tinged with sadness, knowing Jean was now alone." While Shelly and her husband were away, Jean very bravely applied for a job transfer and made plans to relocate in an attempt to start a new life for herself.

There are always problems in the "two-best-friends-plus-one" triangle. It doesn't always add up to three. Some friends survive it beautifully. Others feel they will never find a friendship quite as meaningful. But if that is your attitude, you would also have to assume that you are stuck in a vacuum of time. As you live, you grow and change and you will find other good friends if you are open. That you won't relive the same experience all over again I am sure comes as no surprise. But one cannot travel back in time. Unless one prefers living in past friendships rather than living present ones to the fullest.

Handling the Hurt from Friendship Fallout

This hurt can affect you both ways. Naturally, you will be somewhat sad to leave a friend behind, hoping you haven't hurt him or her. But you, too, can be hurt should a friend leave you behind.

When you are the one who is left, it doesn't feel good. As a matter of fact, it probably feels awful. What can you do? Absorb the hurt, but know that what the other person did at that moment was correct for that person. After all, you've either done the same or wanted to.

The point is that hanging on doesn't work. On either side. And sometimes the honesty of ending is a beautiful and perfect occurrence, even though your ego may be shattered momentarily by the impact. Badmouthing the other person, sulking because you have been rejected, doesn't serve you.

Instead, do this: Close your eyes, see a picture of that person in your mind's eye, pretend you are the other person, and as that other person, write down all the reasons why the friendship is over. Why it's time.

On the other side, if you are the one who has ended the relationship, close your eyes and see the person you have ousted from your life, and frankly and honestly explain to that person why it doesn't work for you anymore. If you live your life totally up front, and by that I mean that you do not disguise your feelings, you may even be able to confront the other in person. But do it only in a spirit of love, not anger. This is possible if you are able to see yourself in a larger-than-life framework, and to examine your own pettinesses as simply part of you, neither good nor bad. We all have pettinesses. I accept mine, and the more I accept them, the more they seem to vanish.

Letting Go Gracefully

There is a time to . . . let go. For if you push a friendship that is wilting, it will die sooner or later. The longer you wait, the less chance you have of ending it gracefully. Remember, too, that letting go means different things. Sometimes you let go of the person you knew, but that person is still on the fringes of your life. You might talk to that person and touch base occasionally because of your shared history and you accept the former friend for what he or she is now. But, you know the person that was and the real friendship have vanished.

A friend of mine says, "To end a friendship, you would have to decide it's costing you more than it's giving you. This is what I mean by costs: There's a cost when a person needs a lot from you but isn't giving anything back. There's a cost when a person will not deal with issues openly and honestly and you see this. There's a cost if you feel the person isn't entirely on your side—for instance, gossiping or saying things behind your back."

We say good-bye when we just don't have enough energy to continue. Maybe at some point we can pick the friendship up again, but right now it doesn't work. You can't just carry all your friendships, good, mediocre, and dying. Life would be too cluttered. For most people it is kinder to reject them than avoid them. It takes a lot of growing and courage to do that and do it well.

Len Snyder, who persistently deals with friendship in his group work, uses an exercise in which he first asks everyone to sit in a circle on the floor, then chooses a person who has been rejected by a friend. That person sits in the center of the circle. He then has that person go around and tell each person where he or she will remember the person—at what stage in their friendship. This is done to get the person to experience deeply why the friendship has been terminated and to see more of his or her own personality at work. Len Snyder feels this is helpful to the disengagement process, an essential part of separation. He feels if you disengage properly, what you are really doing is continuing the friendship process. If you end it in love, you have the option of reactivating the friendship once more or, at least, of having good memories. If you end it in hate, neither is possible.

One patient who understands the importance of friendship much better now said, "Friends are expendable. As I have grown and developed, I've changed my friendships." Snyder says, "I know that my clients are growing as their friendship patterns change. When they first begin, the only kind of people they can relate to are people they really don't see that often. Maybe they go to a movie with them or out for a meal and then come right home. Their other friends are people they work with. Then, a few years later, they're really communicating. They spend a lot of time with friends, talking, being open."

So, letting go of friendships can be seen in another

light. Far from being a hard-hearted act, it is evidence of healthy growth.

To decide, ultimately, whether you should drop a friend, ask yourself this question: Which is more painful—to end a tired relationship or to deceive myself into believing that it still has meaning? or: Does loyalty, habit, or fear hold more meaning than honesty and the courage to say good-bye?

If the questions sound slightly slanted, they are so for a good reason. Most people are so reluctant to end a tired friendship that they often fail to realize the high price they pay when they fail to let go. You might ask yourself some additional questions as well if you find you are undecided.

Ending-a-Friendship Quiz

1. Would you pick this person for your friend if you were just meeting?
2. Does the friendship make you feel alive?
3. Is the friendship worth working at to revitalize it?
4. Are misplaced loyalty, habit or fear the real reasons you can't let go?
5. Are you deceiving yourself by hanging on because you feel the other person would be very hurt?

If your answers to 1–3 are yes, there is no reason to end the friendship. If your answers to 4 and 5 are yes, you might try to make the decision to end the friendship. The beauty of making a clean decision, at least in your mind, that a friendship has ended is that it opens up several positive ways to end it. Coincidentally, these are not unlike the options exercised in ending romantic relationships.

Let's explore the ways to let go:

1. Time

You realize the friendship is over. You *gradually* withdraw from seeing or phoning the person. You don't say anything because you feel it would be kinder and gentler just to "fade out." Probably this is the most popularly used option, but ask yourself if the person wouldn't appreciate a more truthful ending that would leave no room for confusion or curiosity.

2. Gentle Parting

This is a combination of the time factor and perhaps a gentle hint that the relationship is fading. Perhaps you might say, "We've grown in different directions since we met." The emphasis here is on easing out of the friendship as nicely and naturally as possible, but with some preparation. This takes a little work on your part. A little later you may wish to write a note or letter giving reasons for the end of the friendship and wishing the other person well.

3. Confrontation

This consists of a face-to-face final meeting to clear the air and end it. Very few people can do this well, if at all, for obvious reasons. Though confrontation, in this sense of the word, does not mean argument or clash, that is many times exactly what happens. And that is the danger. When it works, it can be a most satisfying and truthful way of ending a friendship. It can also be a way of maintaining personal integrity and a means of personal growth for both people involved.

4. Charity

There are some friends who are too weak to handle an end to a friendship and you know this. Though they may change later, you may, now, be one of their few friends. In this case, rather than hang on out of misplaced kindness, you might end it in kindness. Tell them your intent, give them some time, and help them get adjusted to the loss. For they are not on a level, yet, to realize it might be for the better. For them. Several stages might be passed through—denial, expression of need, sadness and mourning, hostility or depression and, finally, resignation. To accomplish this, you would have to get together and talk it over. Many of us are not used to viewing friendships in quite this fashion, and at first glance, this procedure may seem contrived or odd. But one woman, who was once on the receiving end of this process, realizes now just how well it can work. She had time to adjust and work on her feelings and saw, quite clearly, that each had developed different interests and the relationship was bound to drift apart. She thanked the friend, in the end, for her thoughtfulness and for enabling them both to leave with special feelings and memories.

You can choose your friends but not your relatives. We can leave friends behind but we're usually "stuck" with parents or children. Is it possible to be friends with them?

Chapter VIII
The Real Test of Friendship— Parents and Children

"Mine own familiar friend."

—Psalm XLI

I asked a woman friend whether she felt she had a friendship with her seventeen-year-old daughter. She shook her head slowly. "It is not possible to be friends with your children," she said, "as long as you are taking care of them and paying the bills. Later maybe." This point of view was expressed by several parents who were saying that anything like True-Blue Friendship will occur only when the children are out of the nest and self-supporting. Then it is no longer a one-upsmanship position.

And yet there were parents who defined the True-Blue Friendship differently, and emphatically replied that they are friends with their children and always have been. "Sharing honestly, being who I am as a person not just as a parent, not shielding them from the so-called unpleasant family truths, death, divorce, quarrels, all these things have nurtured it. Yes, we pay the bills, so it is not the complete friendship I might have with another adult, but it certainly is friendship by my definition," one parent said.

In this mobile world where many children have fled their parents by not calling or by disappearing to another part of the country, many parents sit at home in despair, dismay, or guilt, saying, "What did I do wrong?" Now that the storm of family upbringing is over, they would like to be friends but they don't know how.

Parent-child friendship isn't new: Aristotle referred to it in his *Ethics,* Book VIII. He believed that the parent-child friendship is not one between equals, but rather between inferior (child) and superior (parent). Still, he gave it the term *friendship,* but as a "variance" of our usual definition.

Assuming that you want to be friends with your children, young or not so young, what can you do to cement the relationship?

First, be real. Be honest. Be truthful. About yourself. About your feelings for them.

The families I have known in which children talked about sex, showed their angers and fears, and did not regard Mom and Dad as scary authority figures from whom they had to hide, literally and figuratively, have the basis for true friendship.

I talked with children, too, but that will come later.

I remember a dear friend of mine, a writer, who later became a lesbian and told her children the truth. The children, adults now, are heterosexual and among the most functional, happy human beings I know.

The point is that children really know the truth about everything in your life—your sex life, your finances, your relationship with your spouse, the quarrels with the aunts and uncles, and the grandparents—though too many parents pretend that because children happen to be smaller in size than they are, their brains are stunted, too.

Probably just the opposite. Children's antennae are unbelievably keen at picking up all the signals in the household—things you would never suspect. But in the interests of their own survival, they don't tell their parents. They even know when parents use a second language, what those secret words mean. They can sense it; they begin to pick it up. What may happen, in extreme cases, is that if the information they find out is *too* scary for them to handle privately, such as sex, they may eventually deny having that information, even to themselves.

And in those few sentences lie many of the problems that we experience as grown-ups. It is not what we *know* that supposedly hurts us, it is how we interpret it to ourselves that is the kicker.

The gap between children and parents can lessen. In this media age, children are more knowledgeable than they ever have been. They are exposed to all the sophistications of the universe, and yet, many parents still use horse-and-buggy ideas in their parent-child relationships. Shop in this chapter for pointers that both parents and children have shared with me to strengthen the most important human bond. In truth, both parents and children will discover the love we all so desperately seek. And acceptance of who we are as individual human beings.

Can You Be Friends with Your Children?

Marguerite, a divorced mother of a ten-year-old girl, feels it's even more important for the single parent to learn to establish a friendship with her or his children. "I want to be friends with my daughter," Marguerite says frankly. "But I think it's very difficult for parents to be real friends with their children before they are grown up.

"For one thing, we don't have too many interests in common. She's basically interested in three things: her body—meaning any sign of preteen development; the boys in her class; and her Barbie dolls. Those are really burning subjects for her, but they aren't my prime interests. What I'm interested in—my work, my friends, what I'm reading—she's polite about, but she's not vitally interested in, either."

I laughed at Marguerite for taking the interpretation of friendship way too literally. "Interests," those lists we add up, are only a veneer. She does have a good relationship with her daughter and they are friends, at this stage, because Marguerite is close enough to, and talks intimately enough with, her daughter to *know* her. Though she would prefer her daughter to be a bit more scholarly, Elise, at ten, is boy-crazy. I pointed out to her that she accepts her daughter for what she is without expectations. Isn't that part of the friendship between a parent and child?

"Yes, I guess so," she agreed. "But—and here is the most important part—when Elise and I are friendliest is when I leave her alone, which means letting her do what she wants to do and making a lot of her own decisions. But, obviously, I can't do that all the time. So, eventually, it comes back to my telling her to do this or that. Like, I have to ask her if she has brushed her teeth, and tell her to go do it if she hasn't. She resents that and I can understand why. On the other hand, I don't want her to have rotten teeth. A child needs some kind of supervision. And, to me, real friendship cannot exist where one person dominates the other."

It is clear, though, that there is a friendship between mother and daughter. Confirming this was Elise, Marguerite's daughter, who disagreed with her mother. "We are friends," she said, knowing nothing of her mother's comments. "I can tell her what I'm really thinking just like I do with my friends."

Elise wasn't always close to her mother. She used to be Daddy's Little Girl. Now she says, "I see that my mother does a lot of stuff for me and all my father did was buy me things. Now, I'm closer to my mother, but I can be friends with both of them."

"In what ways can you be friends?" I asked.

"Well, with my mother I can talk about personal things. With my father, I can be a 'buddy.' I can play tennis with him and stuff like that."

I asked Elise when she first began to see the difference between her friendship with her mother and that with her father. Was it anything specific one of them did? She hemmed and hawed. Then, she admitted her father was always trying to cuddle her, like a little teddy bear.

"Do you think he still likes to think of you as a baby?" I asked.

"He does and *I hate that!* Like when we go into a store and I want to buy something. I'll say to the man behind the counter, 'Can I have change for a dollar?' because maybe I want to get some bubble gum from the machine. Maybe the guy won't hear me and say, 'What?' Then my father speaks up and asks for me, which really makes me mad. Like I can't do it all by myself."

That might be one lesson in How Not to Plant the Seed of Friendship for a Parent. Supervision is, of course, necessary. Yet, if we can step out from behind our parent role, we may find that children often have an innate wisdom and should be treated with dignity, not as small, helpless objects. Elise's father, when she is twenty-three, may still treat her in much the same way. True feelings of friendship will be sapped by his parental role-playing.

The do's and don't's, should's and shouldn't's have to be decreased as children grow. They are what grown-up children resist.

I am clear that as the child grows older, and if the parent doesn't continue to manipulate the emotional bond by creating dependency, sucking on the relationship and keeping the child from growing up, it is possible for a friendship to grow. This friendship is *not* possible if the child is babied or continuously regiven the tit through gifts.

I found one interesting pattern as I talked to parents and children. Parents often did not believe they were friends with their children but their children felt they were. Ruth and Greg, parents of three children, from preteen to teen, said they didn't think they could ever be friends with their children. Ruth said, "No, you're always a parent."

But her children disagreed. Her middle boy said, enthusiastically, "Yes, I'm friends with my parents. I can talk things over with them. One of my boyfriends heard me use the word 'fuck' in front of my parents. He was shocked. His parents would have killed him. He thought my parents were more like friends than parents." So, it may sometimes be just a matter of definition, words.

I think friendship is *always* possible if parents let go of the "bossy" parent role and just love their children. The secret is so simple. When a child is very young, the parent must be stern about such things as crossing the street without adequate supervision, staying away from the stove, dressing warmly. One psychiatrist whose judgment I value says, "Only those things detrimental to life and limb are to be bossed. Otherwise, nurture a child like a flower. Water it and let it grow!" That advice can form the basis for a friendship that listens, cares, helps, guides but doesn't alienate. Doesn't "play parent."

With friendship comes truth. And there is no reason we can't share some of our truths, maybe all, with our children instead of categorizing certain information as "Not Fit for the Children's Ears." I actually know a worried mother who didn't want her eleven-year-old to know Grandma had been married three times. Again (and again) the truth is—children already know your truths, in the same way parents know when a child is having difficulties or is hiding something. How wearying and untrusting it is to put on that mask all the time, to pretend in front of the children that Daddy's business is not failing when they sense that something is dreadfully wrong. Those lies, or truths, we keep from children can affect their ability to love and trust others. Certainly as children become less and less dependent, much more openness and frankness are possible. It is a case of what the child can absorb about friendship and truth at what age and how gradual the process should be.

Parents who produce children who are friendly toward, as opposed to cold enemies of their parents produce children who will have children who are also friends to *their* parents.

The Terrible Teens

Ideally, the seeds of friendship are planted well before the "terrible" teen years. These are the years when most adolescents understandably rebel, test authority, and try their own wings. Even if those wings are wobbly because they face confusing challenges, they must be tested if they are ever to grow up.

To a parent this is a nerve-shattering time. Children become distant, secretive, moody. More so now than ever before, I think, because we live in a difficult era for teenagers. There are no rules or guidelines. Only peer pressure. There are no taboos, either. When I was a teenager, there wasn't a drug scene or a sex scene. Only a liquor scene. But I do remember what it was like to be a teenager, look like "they" did, act like "they" did. When my son went through his rebellion stage in high school and befriended the prime drug users in school, I knew what it was like to be the parent of a troubled teenager. I thought his friends were grubby, foul-mouthed, lazy, and I did the only thing I felt I could do at the time. I opened my home to them so they had a place to hang out. I fed them, befriended them, listened to their loud music with them. When they burned black holes in my expensive gold carpet with their cigarettes, I must admit I did remind them that it was damned inconsiderate. But I also invited them to come back again and again. I didn't see bad, fresh kids. All I saw were confused, unhappy, floundering adolescents with a frightening array of toys at hand with which to express their rage. I knew they needed warmth and a place to belong. They also needed an adult friend. Many of their parents, upper-middle-class citizens, were shocked and disgusted by their children's unacceptable behavior. As I got to know the boys better, I forgot about my precious gold carpeting. I realized that no possession I owned then or would own was as important as providing something for these confused kids—being there for them.

They were all going through their self-examinations on their way to adulthood in a very dramatic way; that was all. I felt they would come through the crisis. But not if they were rejected by a hostile adult world that judged their actions—smoking pot, cutting school, racing motorcycles—as bad or sick. I knew, at the time, that it was a risk for me, with my own son involved, not to push the firm parental hand that said *Stop*. I also was well aware that I had relinquished authoritative parental control by stepping out of that role and offering friendship. But it was very clear to me that playing the parent role wouldn't help my son.

As I look back, I think I was a little preachy and heavy-handed with the clichéd speeches that began, "I know what you're going through. As a teenager . . ." I was divorced and I asked my ex-husband if he would have a father-son dinner with our son and share with him his own particular teenage problems. I wanted my son to know that a parent is not a god, but likes to keep up the pretense he or she is to maintain dignity.

My son did pull out of his teenage dilemma, as did all the other boys. They are capable young men today. Lawyers, musicians, and doctors. I thought of them recently as I watched my son graduate from law school.

I well remember, also, a father who came to see me because his teenage daughter decided to quit high school. She was a bright girl but going through the typical adolescent upheaval. The father was a big corporation executive so the thought was really upsetting. He could pay for the finest college; in this day and age she could opt for a number of career choices. Suddenly, in the midst of our conversation, the father lowered his head and said, "You know, in a way, this is funny. Nobody knows it, but I quit high school. I went back and finished later. You're the only person I've told. My wife doesn't even know."

I threw back my head and laughed. "Why are you telling me all this?" I asked. "Tell your daughter. Especially what it was like to have to go back and finish high school." He did! She quit anyway. But he shared with his daughter what had become a silly lie.

"Where were you after school?" doesn't work today. Though it is a difficult time for a parent, do not create problems through your disappointment, your expectations. "You're fifteen years old and I can't see where you're going to be anything worthwhile." I can't think of a quicker way *not* to get your child through the teenage years and over the fence to a successful adult life.

It's a rare adolescent who doesn't have some trouble passing through the teen years. It's a wise parent who understands this without guilt or unrealistic expectations. And extends the hand of friendship.

If psychological help is needed for a troubled teenager, I would not hesitate to see a counselor of some sort, but I do feel the most far-reaching assistance comes from counseling in which the whole family participates; in which the family is guided into telling truths they might have had difficulty expressing.

Sex Instead of Candy Bars

Because the subject of this book is Friendship, I have avoided the issue of sex. But I do think it belongs in this chapter for a reason. It seems to me that early sexual experiences, as available as the candy bars our kids once wanted at the local drugstore, may hinder rather than help the formation of friendships.

We have gone from the problem of repressed sexuality of generations ago to easy sexual encounters and the current emphasis on sex. There's peer pressure placed on children to be sexually active.

When sex is solely for sex's sake, there is no continuity. Bodies meet but often there is an alienation in the heart. Many adults can handle this and enjoy the sex. In the teen years, when it is often scary to reveal any kind of truths about yourself—who you are, what you are—when you may not even know some of the answers, it can be frightening to sample and discard sex partners like the candy in a trick-or-treat bag.

What do you tell your teenagers? In this era, forbidding your kids to have sex until marriage is laughably old-fashioned and out of sync. I can't think of a quicker way to tempt them. But you might very well have a sincere conversation in which you point out that the teenage years are a time for forming real friendships. That a series of quick sexual encounters, without friendship, without two people really *knowing* each other, is adding a lot of unnecessary hurt to a most crucial stage of life.

Today it is both the girl *and* the boy who may be suddenly rejected after a few sexual experiences. I am unwilling any longer to postulate that it is "worse" for the girl. As we liberate men, we begin to discover that they have the same sensitive feelings women have, and although a girl has the added risk of pregnancy, I think, in light of easily available contraception and our changing times, the notion that the girl is more likely to be upset by sex and rejection is an antiquated one, indeed.

Teenagers want to feel they *belong*. With sex, they may feel they do. But the rejection that is inevitable in teenage romances may become sexual rejection as well. And I think that's far too complicated when they are still trying to answer the question—Who am I?

Bad-Influence Friends

Every parent has at some time wished a friend out of a child's life. How can a sensible kid pick such a friend, so obviously a bad influence? What can you do? If you badmouth this friend, won't it guarantee a deeper friendship?

It may help to understand that sometimes children

choose friends who reflect the unexpressed part of themselves. The bad child who does and says things the good little child wouldn't dream of doing or saying provides a way of rebelling against parents. Children become friends with someone who will rebel for them.

What can you do when your child selects a friend, or friends, you consider unsuitable? Don't forget the notion of "unsuitable" is yours, not your child's. I have known intellectual parents concerned because their children had rock-and-roll friends rather than studious ones. Certainly teenagers select friends out of a deep need to be loved and accepted. They choose other kids with whom they can share their innermost feelings at a time in life when those deep feelings are simply bursting to be let out. Choosing friends is a human right, and the parent may not necessarily like the choice.

But what if you discover that your child is friendly with someone you feel is a *truly* destructive influence? You might sit down and ask some questions. Not like an FBI agent, but in the spirit of finding out more about the friend and the friendship. Here are some sample questions you might ask to get you started.

Why do you like your friend?
What do you get from the friendship?
Do you have other friends you like as well?
Do they get along with your friend?
Do you think this person is fun to be with?

And you might add, "I am trying not to dislike your friend, but he or she does do such-and-such. Could you help me get a better picture so I can like him or her, too?" Remember, don't judge! And know that friendships can shift as rapidly in a child's life as interests. It is a wise parent who can distinguish beween a *better* friend and a merely *different* one.

Hi, Mom, Hi, Dad—I Want You to Know I'm Gay

A couple in their forties received a phone call this summer. Their youngest child, living in New York, called to "come out of the closet." He told them he was gay, had been for years, and invited them to come to New York and stay with him—and his roommate-lover.

His parents were shocked. They had had no idea. They were upset and confused but they decided to accept their son's offer of friendship. They wanted their only son as a friend.

It used to be that we read about or saw gays only in Greenwich Village in New York City or in places like Miami or California. They were invisible elsewhere, probably because it was necessary for survival for many homosexuals, men and women, to stay securely in the closet. Now they're coming out honestly. Many middle-class parents are getting phone calls or visits from children who say, "I want you to know I'm gay." I think this is an act of courage. And an act of love. The children want to live truthful lives and they want to be friends with their parents. For this I applaud them. I still remember the era when the single aunt or uncle came to visit. Everybody "knew" but no one discussed it.

But what of the parents? Can they accept their son or daughter's open admission of homosexuality? Can they be friends with their child? It is possible. I have a friend with whom I went to lunch when I was in California. As we arrived at the restaurant, she told me she had taken her daughter there for lunch the other day to console her over her recent separation from a lover. The lover was a woman.

To be friends with a child who says he or she is gay and wants to be friends, I think parents have to let go of past expectations, old beliefs about the way we are "supposed" to lead our lives and just accept. What I mean by expectations are those ideas to which we become attached to nourish our own egos. This one will be a lawyer. That one will be a doctor. They will marry very well. Everyone expects a child to be heterosexual; there isn't another thought. But if a child turns out to be homosexual, I would throw away the psychological analyzing, the blaming, the guilts, and just look at the child. Is he or she happy in life? And love them for what they are *now*.

Friends for Life

After children grow up, the friendship between parent and child can really blossom. It can become one of equality. The controls have been eased, the children are trusted and respected as people. Janice, a mother of two, admits, "Being a mother is being a super-personality and letting go of that makes friendship possible."

Author Eileen Dent has a beautiful friendship with her two daughters, now in their mid-twenties.

She says, "The truth is I didn't set out to do anything. Didn't really plan on this friendship when they got older. It just evolved. I do feel you're always a parent, but if you don't relate to your children after a certain age only as a parent, you begin to relate to them on a one-to-one basis as you would anyone else. In fact, I dedicated a book to them and I said in it, 'To Roxanne Elizabeth and Karen

Susan with love and friendship, always.' This was a natural thing for me to say.

"I had a male friend who said to me, 'I don't know. I don't believe that parents should be friends with their children because they lose respect for you.' So, I said, 'Well, what's more important to you, respect given in fear, because that's really all you're saying to me, or love that is friendship.' And he said, 'I'd rather have respect.' And I really felt very sorry for him. Because he isn't going to get either."

Is It Possible to Be Friends with Your Parents?

Joan Rivers used to tell a joke in her monologue. During a family Thanksgiving dinner, she went up to the bathroom to sneak a cigarette away from her mother's eyes. She bumped into her mother, in the bathroom, sneaking a cigarette away from *her* mother's eyes.

The audience laughed. They recognized the fact that some parents are simply unable or unwilling to give up the parent role. The child may be an adult with his or her own children, and still the parent is telling the child what to do.

Some children try hard to fight it: "Listen, Ma, I'm thirty-two and I've earned my own living for ten years. I feel I have a right to live my life the way I want. I don't want to eat my mashed potatoes."

If something like this is said in love and not rancor, it may do the trick. But not always. Some parents will simply dig harder into the parent role.

One young woman, a twenty-nine-year-old successful graphics designer, had negative feelings about friendship

with her mother. "I would like to be friends with my
mother but I can't. She sits in judgment on everyone and
everything. She hasn't met a man I've been interested in
since I've been sixteen, and she never will. She pulls each
one apart. She would pull Robert Redford apart if he
walked through the door. No one would be right.

"I try to see her as little as I can and say as little as I can
about myself. But I love her anyway!"

There *are* some parents who simply will not let their
children be—and so the child withdraws. I would have to
take the side of the young person who rightfully demands
his or her own autonomy. We are each entitled to live our
own lives, make our own mistakes and enjoy our own
good fortunes. Without constantly being directed by our
parents.

We have all known parents who had a grip on their
children at age forty, fifty, or even sixty. I remember the
fascinating documentary film *Grey Gardens,* about Jackie
Onassis's eccentric cousin, Edith Beale, who lived in an
unkempt house, condemned by the community of East
Hampton, New York. With her lived her fifty-year-old
daughter, Little Edie, who had once broken away from
home to pursue a career in Manhattan but had returned
to Mama, who pulled all the strings and manipulated her
emotions as if she were a puppet. I would not call mothers
and daughters with that kind of close relationship friends.

Friendship is possible, though, between most parents
and children. Francine, an office manager of twenty-
eight, feels she has finally reached the point where her
mother is a friend. Almost. The reservations in their
friendship occur whenever anything alluding to her so-
called "swinging singles sex life" pops up. They do not
discuss it. Francine says she thinks her mother would not
approve of more than one man. Many other young women
also don't share experiences with mothers who don't ap-

prove of sex unless one is married. The mothers might very well suspect it exists, but they don't want it spelled out.

This would be amusing, but many young women are still torn by the guilt their mothers' silent disapproval can bring. When I indicated to Francine that perhaps her mother was jealous, she repeated, "Jealous! Of what?" Then it occurred to her. Her mother had never had the opportunity to live her life as freely as Francine was living hers. And Mother was too used to avoiding the subject to admit she regretted it, maybe even to herself.

The same is true for fathers as well. What father didn't have the fantasy, twenty to twenty-five years ago, of living with a couple of different women without the pressure of settling down? Or maybe not having to marry at all?

Now there's his son doing just that, and they're all nice girls, too. One side of Pop's mind is urging his son to settle down and the other side is secretly wishing he could have lived the same way.

One may say that it's not possible to be friends with your parents if you haven't grown up with them in friendship. It's too late. But I disagree. Forget right now about trying to change a sixty-year-old mother or father. Learn to meet them halfway in friendship.

How to Be Friends with Your Parents

I happen to feel that total separation between parents and children is one of the great tragedies of our culture. Both generations really need the sustenance the other has to give and both are impoverished when the relationship does not continue. It doesn't matter, either, if you live thousands of miles away. You are not separate if you have maintained the love in your heart; it is important to *your* growth. Because if you harbor ill-will toward your parents, I think you have disowned part of yourself.

When you hate a parent, you hate part of yourself; when you are not friends with a parent, you are not friends with an aspect of yourself. These are tough words, but I see so clearly that the heart is whole only when one's relationship with oneself is whole.

And that means coming to terms with your childhood, with whatever you thought you should have gotten from your parents—love, education, whatever. Everyone has a different item of insufficiency, beginning with the phrase, "if only it had been different." The truth is, it wasn't. Every single one of us has lived a human personal drama in a family; some appear to be in a slot better than others. But there is no point in kicking yours. Some traumas made bigger dents in some people's psyches. If yours are simply the ordinary resentments, give them up. Know that they, your mommy and daddy, did what they did with the only information they had then.

Being friends with your parents is first accepting and loving them in your heart. Second, it is maintaining whatever contact works for you. If you can only phone once a month, do that. If you can stop by once a week, do that. There are no rules. None at all.

But when the emotional distance has been great, you may ask, how can you try to be friends with your parents? Be truthful. Go to a parent as a loving friend. Say, "This is me and this is what I am and this is what I stand for." They probably know anyway.

A young woman came to me and said, "How can I tell my mom and dad I went on my vacation with a man? They'd have a heart attack!" I'm not so sure. I would say it would be better to tell the truth and try to establish friendship. Give up the need for your parents' approval and you will be free to be friends.

Here's a speech you might try:

> Mother, Dad, I'd like to talk to you. I want to be
> friends with you. So, I'd like to say I've been living
> with someone for two years. And, yes, I've kept it
> secret from you. We may or may not marry. This is
> our lifestyle. I'm happy, also, in my career. I know
> you wanted something else for me, but this is what
> I am now.

You could break that speech up and let it spill out in
your conversation, too. Talk the truth. It will go a long
way in friendship. Especially if you do not blame your
parents for what they did or did not do for you.

And here's another speech that will go further:

> Mother, Dad, I've wondered for a long time how
> you really are. I'd like us to be friends. Are you
> really happy now that I've grown up? What is your
> life like? What kinds of things do you do?

Keep asking them about themselves. Remember,
friendship requires a good listener. To expect them always to listen to you and your problems is to expect them
always to play their parent role.

Many of us are friendlier with surrogate parents than
we are with our own parents. There's a certain bond between aunt, uncle, nephew, niece. I even know one
woman who turned her next-door neighbor, a wonderful
and warm woman, into a surrogate mother. Perhaps you
can think of your natural parents as surrogate parents—
the ones we like because we can be ourselves with them.

I can't think of a more beautiful celebration of friendship than for parents and children to come together as
friends instead of facing each other across the battlelines.
I think this is an area where many problems can be solved.
And there are other ways of celebrating friendship, as
well.

Chapter IX
Celebrations of Friendship

"The man who thinks he can live without others is mistaken; the one who thinks others can't live without him is even more deluded."

—Hasidic saying

I loved reading what Francine du Plessix Gray said in her Barnard College commencement speech of 1978. Reflecting on the reasons she had chosen friendship as her topic, she said, "In a world more and more polluted by the lying of politicians and the illusions of the media, I occasionally crave to hear and tell the truth. To borrow a beautiful phrase from Friedrich Nietzche, I look upon my friend as 'the beautiful enemy' who alone is able to offer me total candor. Friendship is by its very nature freer of deceit than any other relationship we can know because it is the bond least affected by striving for power, physical pleasure, or material profit, most liberated from any oath of duty or of constancy." She went on to say that with *eros* our body stands naked, but with friendship our spirit stands naked.

The real you is exposed in friendship. No wonder so many people lack friends and have trouble finding them. No wonder millions of us complain of aching loneliness.

You Need Never Be Lonely Again

Loneliness is friendship's shadowy underside. I think this poem expresses what so many of us might feel or sense:

I saw in Louisiana, a live-oak growing,
All alone stood it, and the moss hung down from the
* branches,*
Without any companion it grew there, uttering
* joyous leaves of dark green,*
And its look, rude, unbending, lusty, made me think
* of myself,*
But I wondered how it could utter joyous leaves,
* standing alone there, without its friend, its lover*
* near—for I knew I could not,*
And I broke off a twig with a certain number of
* leaves upon it, and twined around it a little moss,*
And brought it away—and I have placed it in sight
* in my room,*
It is not needed to remind me as of my own dear
* friends,*
(For I believe lately I think of little else than of
* them,)*
Yet it remains to me a curious token—it makes me
* think of manly love;*
For all that, and though the live-oak glistens there
* in Louisiana, solitary, in a wide flat space,*
Uttering joyous leaves all its life, without a friend, a
* lover, near,*
I know very well I could not.

—Walt Whitman

Even animals feel lonely without people. When Southern California's Marineland closed temporarily for remodeling, the dolphins sulked, the sea lions overate, and the killer whales became depressed. They were . . . lonely. They missed the people who had filled the bleachers. In order to ease the animals' feelings of separateness, groups of local schoolchildren were invited to free shows in the park twice a week until the reopening.

I am convinced that without friends we would all wither and eventually die. I am thinking of older people, who live on alone in a half-death after their friends are gone.

Babies need more than a change of diapers and a bottle. They also need the nourishment provided by cuddling, kissing and tenderness. As adults we need our share of stroking, emotional and mental. We need the approval and even disapproval of friends. Unlike animals and babies, we can be shown ways to satisfy this need.

One young man I know who has several friends unwittingly became part of a personal experiment that taught him a lot about loneliness. He had exams to pass, and taking a calendar, he drew up a rigid schedule, one that left no room for "goofing off" or any kind of social life. In his zeal to study, he decided to cut out all time spent with his friends. He survived on this schedule for only a week when he confessed, "I simply went bananas. What a mistake I made. I was depressed. I couldn't study anymore. The one thing I did need were my friends. They are very supportive, and when my support is cut off, I feel terribly lonely." He revised his priorities to allow time for friends—for life and love and warmth.

I no longer find it amazing to pick up the personals section of many newspapers and see that advertisers are not only looking for a mate, but they are also looking for friends. What a true commentary on our times! Can you imagine fifty years ago, or even twenty-five, having to advertise for companionship? It may be an alternate way of meeting people, and do it if you need to. However, it probably won't cure your loneliness. Only *you* can do that.

Professor William Sandler, Jr., author of *Existence and Love*, and sociology professor at Bloomfield College in New Jersey, cautions us not to feel harassed by our loneliness. "It may be a sign of strength of character," he adds. "It is not necessarily to be thought of as a character deficiency or form of self-pity. Look at the great men and women in world history who have frequently expressed a deep loneliness—scientists, artists, religious leaders. A great person with an original idea will experience loneliness because he or she can't communicate it."

Communication. That's the key word for everyone, famous or not, who suffers from loneliness, whether temporarily or terminally. And everyone is lonely sometimes! But it's not good enough to chat or share our views. We need to learn to communicate on a *feeling level*. We tend to conceal our feelings because we do not want another person to sense our vulnerability. Boys are taught, "Don't cry, don't show that it hurts." Girls are taught, "Don't show that you want something very much." It's all a vicious circle. *When you become an expert at concealing, then you can't communicate on a feeling level very effectively. When you don't communicate with someone on a feeling level, then you experience loneliness.*

Professor Sadler feels people need skills to show them how to be more open, take risks and experience rejection without feeling humiliated. In his loneliness workshops, participants do exercises in which they allow themselves to feel vulnerable through role-playing. They are then given help to practice becoming more open. Loneliness cannot be cured with a do-it-yourself kit.

Perhaps not. But those who are lonely must begin somewhere or remain feeling isolated. We must try to slip out of that dark cave of loneliness by ourselves, if we have to. The only way to do that is to keep in mind that we are not alone, after all. In the popular growth movements such as est, Actualizations, Insight, Zen, and Chareeva, people are realizing that dissatisfaction, fear and emptiness stem from the illusion that we are separate. In these new trainings, people get the opportunity to lift the layers of their personalities and know they are *not* separate. We are all One.

That great psychic pain we feel is the illusion of separation. It gives us a darkened view of the world rather than a joyful one. Every single one of us has the potential to love others and ourselves. This potential has merely been blocked by learned habits of separateness.

Your possibilities for friendship are endless. Loneliness does not have to be in your life unless you choose to have it there. The do-it-yourself cure for you, without benefit of a workshop or participation in a group movement, is simply to get out there and become part of the human scene. Forget about the reasons you may have become blocked, the alleged damage done to you as a child—that was, after all, so long ago. Simply approach each new moment in your life as a possibility for friendship. The miracle is that a person will be out there wanting your gift of friendship. He or she is willing to accept you as you are and is delighted that you exist. That is as good a beginning as any for easing loneliness out of your life. For if just one person is there and you make an effort to be open, in time many will be there.

Rituals of Friendship

I wanted to discover some new rituals of friendship. I was looking for some sort of symbolism like that found in romance, perhaps candy and flowers and diamond rings.

In almost every Western I'd ever seen, Indians exchanged the peace pipe or ceremoniously became "blood brothers." I recalled the antics of fraternity initiates who had done everything from swallowing goldfish to painting fraternity letters on a rock overlooking a highway. Some of these pranks had even been highly dangerous. I remembered, too, girls in the fifties who wore hearts on a long chain to symbolize they were best friends. Each wore half a heart, which would fit only the other half worn by her friend. Beyond that, I really couldn't find obvious rituals. Old or new.

I know this is not so in other societies and cultures. Friendship among the Polynesian Tikopia of the Pacific islands is celebrated throughout their lives, cemented by reciprocal obligations and the constant exchange of gifts. In Africa, the Bangwa sing the praises of their friends. One could go on forever, anthropologically, with similar experiences and examples, but let's put the exotic places and hard-to-pronounce names aside. We might conclude, though, that our society may be the only culture that does not really celebrate friendship.

Children still have rituals of friendship. These are played out with games and rhymes. Young children take friendship very seriously, playing imaginary but intense games, exchanging dolls, stamps, trading cards. Some children follow a ritual of inventing an imaginary friend and for a long time Susie or Tommy may be very real to them, even acknowledged by their parents.

Children make and break friendships with surprising speed. Anthropologist Robert Brain describes in his book *Friends and Lovers* children's rituals in England, where a symbol of close friendship is interlocking the little fingers. The fingers are linked, shaken up and down, and the friends recite:

Make friends, make friends,
Never, never break friends.

If they quarrel, this ritual must be amended by chanting:

Break friends, break friends,
Never, never make friends.

If they make up again, they moisten the little fingers and say:

We've broken before,
We break now.

Separating the little fingers, the following ritual is added:

Make up, make up,
Never row again,
If we do we'll get the cane.

Then they intertwine their moistened fingers and squeeze tightly. Or they might seal their bond by slapping hands or smacking each other.

In America, little girls of ten, who are growing up fast enough to merit an anthropological study all their own, exchange "Boy Books." Elise explains what this signifies:

"We don't exchange things so much as we exchange words. Like we have these notebooks we write in. There's 'What boy do you love the best in the class?' 'Who's the handsomest?' Even, 'Who's the ugliest boy?' Then we all answer the questions."

Scott, a seventeen-year-old from Cleveland, feels the most ritualistic trend among boys and girls of his age group is the tendency to have groups of male and female friends rather than the much publicized one-to-one teen-age dating relationship. He feels all the dating and heavy sex belong to the previous era of teens. On a recent group tour of teenagers to Israel, he found boys and girls from the South, Midwest, East, and Canada were much the same. Though there are still teenagers who place great importance on dating, become involved with sex and drugs, he feels this stereotyped image of the typical teenager is passé. He does feel there's a new importance placed on friendship or what teenagers of a much earlier era called "hanging out."

I would like to relate a very special story. It is about the mother of a friend of mine. The mother is eighty-one. We would all imagine, I am sure, a stereotypical old woman's life. A lonely, quiet existence. One in which she looks forward to contact with her children as her only communication.

Not so with this woman, as you will quickly see. Frieda has fourteen friends she can call at any hour of the day or night. She has lived in Philadelphia for sixty of her eighty-one years and, fortunately, most of her contemporaries are still living.

I'm sure her story is exceptional, yet it proves that friendship has no age limit and provides a hopeful goal for us all. Frieda says, "I have tremendous tolerance for being alone. But you don't know what it is like to wake up in bed in the middle of the night in a large apartment building and know you can telephone any one of many friends who live close by, just to make contact. We, none of us, sleep so well, so we have an unwritten pact that it is all right to telephone. Any time.

"That is what makes it possible for me to live alone.

"When we are out together we do *not* talk about old times, our children or our grandchildren. Rather we talk about politics, ecology, or other current events. We go on excursions to museums or have coffee at a small coffee house and watch the parade of young people.

"I don't know when we actually decided not to talk about our children as we got older—but no one does.

"Because of my friends, I am still enthusiastic about each day, even though my hearing is going rapidly. I am in excellent health otherwise, and walk five miles a day. And every single day I do something with a friend. Mostly our conversation is about what we are doing right this minute."

Frieda, living remarkably in the present, is also an example of what is becoming a form of friendship ritual for adults. Or, at least, we are lately classifying it as one. For while our society doesn't smoke peace pipes or follow formalized friendship rituals, we do have ways to celebrate it.

The Intimacy Network

A little like the communes that sprang to life in the sixties are the little families people like Frieda are forming. They are quite successful and important to survival. Some describe them as Intimacy Networks. An Intimacy Network is, simply, an informal group of people, generally not related by blood ties, who pledge, nevertheless, to support one another emotionally, to be with one another in times of emergency, and to enjoy one another's good company in times of leisure.

An Intimacy Network might get started in an apartment building, in a neighborhood, in a city or suburb. One of its necessary ingredients is physical proximity, just as it used to be in the neighborhoods of long ago. It's the nearness and constant contact that feed the closeness.

Some people in an Intimacy Network, obviously, may even be having sexual relations. But that is *not* the important part, strange as it may seem to some. It's the friendship that counts.

We have come to associate the word *network* with television stations, secret societies, and a hodgepodge of wires and poles. In reality, we are speaking of families. Families of friends.

Clans, Tribes, Families

Author Jane Howard, writing on this subject in her book *Families*, says:

> The trouble with the clans and tribes many of us were born into is not that they consist of meddlesome ogres but that they are too far away. In emergencies we rush across continents and if need be oceans to their sides, as they do to ours. Maybe we even make a habit of seeing them, once or twice a year, for the sheer pleasure of it. But blood ties seldom dictate our addresses. Our blood kin are often too remote to ease us from our Tuesdays to our Wednesdays. For this we must rely on our families of friends. If our relatives are not, do not wish to be, or for whatever reasons cannot be our friends, then by some complex alchemy we must try to transform our friends into our relatives. If blood and roots don't do the job, then we must look to water and branches, and sort ourselves into new constellations, new families.

Howard believes these families of friends may consist of "friends of the road" (chance friends), or "friends of the heart" (choice friends).

One young woman I know found a greeting card she thought was especially appropriate for an older woman who had been a friend to her. It was lettered, "Happy Surrogate Mother's Day." She mailed it to thank this woman for including her in family holidays.

We need not confine our tribes or families or clans to anyone's blood relatives. Most families of friends are not blood-related. I remember once watching a neighbor getting ready to visit a group of single friends on an otherwise lonely Sunday afternoon. A twinkle came into her eyes as she spoke of the close group she belonged to. "We're like a family."

You may belong to a family, or even more than one network, of friends who group and gather together. If you do not belong to such a group right now, the beauty comes in recognizing that they are out there, they do exist, and you can help in creating one anytime you wish. Through one friend who links you to other friends, you can belong to a family. It is much easier to do this now than at any other time in history. Traditionally, most people belonged to the nuclear family. Now, people are comfortably joining, gravitating to, and inventing their own groups. Creating their own families.

When this happens, you will discover certain rituals. They need not be formalized rituals such as cooking a big turkey on Thanksgiving or exchanging gifts on Christmas Day. The rituals will be spontaneous and special to your group and will spring from the moment they happen (though you may value their significance only in retrospect). A certain dinner to celebrate a nontraditional holiday—the anniversary of the day the group did its first "anything." Do you see what I mean? I do not think the rituals for modern friendship can be formalized, and that makes it quite interesting, when you stop to think about it.

Also interesting is what's happening to our love/romance rituals. Friendship expressions are being felt. Look at all the new, inventive wedding ceremonies that promise not to "love, honor and *obey*" but are as way out as "for as long as we both shall dig each other." One day, when I began this book, I was sitting in the garden of a city restaurant, the delighted observer of the wedding of two young people, which I could see from a distance.

I heard the minister ask, after the couple had been declared man and wife, the following: "Will you, as friends and relatives of this couple, do all you can within your power to help them uphold these vows?" And then he added, "Let all married persons who have witnessed these vows be strengthened in their own."

It seemed to me such a beautiful example of extending the role of friendship to include assisting the couple and the guests to stay together in our society with its high divorce rate, a statistic that overshadows the flowery, old-fashioned wedding rituals. This friendship ritual, I understand, is part of the new ceremony of the Episcopal Church.

Can We Celebrate Friendship?

With no reassuring rituals, a vague yearning to belong somewhere, a nationwide epidemic of loneliness, and people all around us who still take friendship for granted—can we honestly *celebrate* friendship?

Yes, we can do it every day. Those one-line popular friendship cards, very carefully crafted by psychologists to say what we feel but can't say, don't have to do it for us. We can do it for ourselves.

Let me tell you my Wedding Shower Story. My friend Marion described it, enthusiastically, as the most unusual wedding shower in the whole United States.

She was adding the usual festive touches, setting out her best table linen, polishing her coffeepot, extending streamers from the centerpiece, when suddenly she got a cold chill. Trying to figure out why, she came up with

this. Her body was performing loving actions, but her
mind, if she was perfectly truthful with herself, was not.
She admitted she was terribly, though maybe irrationally,
jealous of her best friend who had a loving, warm relationship with her husband-to-be. Marion was divorced,
alone. Part of her was delighted for her friend; part of her
was furious that she was deprived of the same joy. All the
elegance of the table, even the frosting on the cake,
seemed to mock her. "I knew, then," she says, "that I
actually hated her for her happiness. I was slightly ap-
palled at my inner mind for revealing this kind of spoil-
sport information to me."

When they sat on the floor, for the customary gift-
opening, Marion got a bright idea.

" 'Listen,' I said, 'let's just stop for a moment and share
our true feelings about Suzanne's shower.' My face felt
beet red and it was one of the hardest things I've ever
done, but I couldn't stop. I blurted out my true feeling.
'I'm happy for Suzanne, but the truth is, I'm also horribly
jealous.' "

A hush fell over the room then and Marion didn't know
what to think.

Then one by one, the chorus of shared feelings came
through. Forty women were present at that shower.
Though not all had cause to feel jealousy, one by one those
who recognized the same truth chimed in, "So am I! I feel
the same way!" Each woman shared her honest feelings
and it was truly a marvelous, supportive sharing. The
women laughed and cheered and wept. The married
women shared their truths about marriage. It was an un-
forgettable evening for all of them. Everyone rejoiced in
Suzanne's shower in her own way, not the way of the traditional shower. As Marion told it to me, she said, "I will
treasure it to remember that when truth comes out, joy
comes with it."

So, this is a very important lesson about friendship: *We can celebrate it every day with truth.*

If we can celebrate with truth, then we can celebrate by expressing anger with our friends rather than holding back. Or as poet William Blake once wrote, "I was angry with my friend: I told my wrath, my wrath did end."

Here is, I think, another way to celebrate friendship. I recently wrote a note to a dear friend. It came out of my est experience and because of my thinking about friendship.

It said:

> Dear Craig—For many years now you have been like a father to my son. I know he has always appreciated it. But I've never said how much I have as well. So, I'm saying it now. After all these years. Because, if I don't tell you, how will you know?

That's the point. *If I don't tell you, how will you know?* How do any of us know unless someone tells us or we tell someone? Think of how many times, maybe even quite recently, you didn't tell someone that you liked her outfit, that you admired a special talent she had, that you thought he had really "gotten it together" of late? How many of us are too busy, too tongue-tied, too embarrassed or shy to voice such honest compliments? But part of the celebration of friendship and an exercise in communicating on a feeling level is learning to recognize and release the reins we hold on our emotions and being "quick on the trigger" to express freely what we are feeling at the moment. This does not mean doling out an unfelt compliment a day or using a slick apple-polishing technique most intelligent people can see through. It means simply—if I don't tell you, how will you know?

I do think, since we must all be guilty of taking friend-

ship (at least sometime in our lives) for granted that the
best celebration of friendship, right now, is . . . *to be
aware of it.* That means understanding it. Knowing its
joys. Not being afraid of its risks. Learning to be ourselves
and open up so we can be a friend and have friends. To
celebrate this every day, keep in mind the basic ideas
culled from this book that were donated from the hearts
and minds of all the people who shared with me what
friendship means to them.

   If you could carry this book in a little memory bank,
like computers have, what would be important to have in
this imaginary file folder to help you celebrate the friendships in your life? Just this:

> Don't take friendship for granted.
>
> Remember, loneliness occurs when *you* don't com-
> municate on a feeling level.
>
> Know the difference between an acquaintance and a
> friend, and when you don't confuse the two you
> won't feel hurt.
>
> Know what being a True-Blue Friend means.
>
> Get out and be part of the world. Launch a campaign,
> anytime you have to, to find friends, and after a while
> they will find you.
>
> Know that you need many types of friends in your
> life. No one friend can possess *everything.*
>
> Know the importance of having friends other than
> your beloved.
>
> Understand how and who to go to for a friend-thera-
> pist.
>
> Know when you are playing a "controlling" or a "con-
> trolled" role in a friendship and how to balance the
> scale.

Know the "different" friendship between children
and parents. Explore and experience it.
Realize it's no sin to terminate a friendship and learn
how to do it gracefully.
Celebrate, when you can, with a family of friends.

I feel that friendship has never been more necessary or
more welcome than right now. For years, there has been
tremendous emphasis on man's aggressive instincts, his
urge to kill, fight, be separate. No one, on the other hand,
has quite so dramatized or promoted man's desire to love
and share.

Sigmund Freud himself actually *denied* our basic need
for love and friendship. He believed our coming together
as social animals to be nothing more than the overcoming
of sexual jealousy. Hate was recognized as a more spontaneous urge than love. Interests such as art, literature,
and music were classified as a sublimation of sexual energy.

I realize I touch on an area of controversy here, but the
fact is—it just doesn't wash. Many experts in the field
now realize that, though Freud was the Father of Psychoanalysis, he was also a product of his age and this colored
some of his theories. Many of his ideas fit the nineteenth-
century middle-class culture in which he lived. Modern-
day feminists would agree his theories on women's capa-
bilities, or incapabilities, are based on a limited, histori-
cally biased perception of the female sex. Since Freud
lived in the Age of Individualism, he naturally placed
much emphasis on survival of the fittest, self-reliance, the
separation of man from man.

That all belongs to yesterday. The human potential
movement that burgeoned in the 1960s with trainings and
experiences has assisted people to reach inside and ex-

press love to one another. Contemporary physics tells us that we are merely compressed energy systems and the empty space between us is also energy. In logic, too, we are all linked together. *We are all one.*

Melanie Klein, famed psychoanalyst, post-Freudian, and author of *Envy and Gratitude* and *The Psychoanalysis of Children*, among other works, assures us that without love a child cannot have a sense of identity. That there is no peace of mind possible without feeling and expressing love. As we grow into adults, we have friends and express love. Our sexual drives are simply that, and they take a back seat to the feelings of friendship and love.

Studies of primitive cultures show that "cooperation" between members of these small societies, along with tolerance of outsiders, is more the rule than the exception. They also suggest that primitive people are *not* prone to constant aggression and external violence unless they are at war. They further suggest that we have accepted the universal myth that aggression and hate are natural to human beings to excuse our involvement in genocide and war, not to mention our modern obsession with violence.

No matter what anthropological theory you embrace, though, perhaps this is the most measured comment of all: We now know that man has a tremendous capacity for sharing, friendship and love.

Those who are lonely feel deprived. We are moving away from that Era of Separateness and into the Age of Cooperation. We look to friendship for our feelings of *security and a sense of roots*.

Try this simple exercise: Look back on any day of your life. It could have been last year or yesterday. Pick one that stands out as being especially joyous or memorably awful. Odds are, no matter what the events were, the good day was one in which you felt close and warm and loving to a person or to people. The disastrous day was one in which you felt separate, deciding you were really all alone.

I'd like to add just one more definition of friendship. It goes like this; Friendship is the capacity of two human beings to be with each other in caring and sharing with honesty.

I suggest that the way to do this is to be the one to take off your mask first, to be who you are, not pretend to be who you are not. And that one by one, as the barriers to your open communication are eradicated, you and I can be who we were truly meant to be. Loving friends.

Index